TOGETHER WITH TECHNOLOGY

Writing Review, Enculturation, and Technological Mediation

Jason Swarts
North Carolina University

Baywood's Technical Communications Series
Series Editor: CHARLES H. SIDES

Routledge
Taylor & Francis Group

LONDON AND NEW YORK

First published 2008 by Baywood Publishing Company, Inc.

2 Park Square, Milton Park, Abingdon, Oxon OX14 4RN
711 Third Avenue, New York, NY 10017, USA

Routledge is an imprint of the Taylor & Francis Group, an informa business

First issued in paperback 2017

Library of Congress Catalog Number: 2007008587
ISBN 13: 978-0-89503-362-8 (hbk)

Library of Congress Cataloging-in-Publication Data

Swarts, Jason, 1972-
    Together with technology : writing review, enculturation, and technological mediation / by Jason Swarts.
        p.   cm. -- (Baywood's technical communications series)
    Includes bibliographical references and index.
    ISBN 978-0-89503-362-8 (cloth : alk. paper) 1. Authorship--Collaboration--Data processing. 2. Editing--Data processing. 3. Information technology--Social aspects. I. Title. II. Title: Writing review, enculturation, and technological mediation.

PN171.D37S83 2007
808' . 027--dc22   2007008587

ISBN 978-0-89503-362-8 (hbk)
ISBN 978-0-415-78373-6 (pbk)

Table of Contents

Introduction

People rarely go through the day without encountering texts. These texts include the mundane (e.g., receipts, to-do lists, bills) and the specialized (e.g., progress reports, procedures manuals, patient histories). All help form the basis of our social and professional activities by providing us with structured information needed to act in the world. Texts clarify and structure tasks in which they are used, which is to say that they "mediate" (Hutchins, 1997, p. 338) and become part of the environments in which we carry out physical and cognitive activities. Treatment rooms, classrooms, and offices are the names that describe the configurations of technology, texts, and people in those spaces. We learn to participate in these text-rich settings easily enough, as we become more aware of the activities they mediate. Imagine a simple example of buying concert tickets at a ticket counter. Based on the cues that we read in the design of the ticket counter, we know how to complete a transaction (i.e., where to speak, stand, put our money). Also, on the ticket counter are price lists, accepted forms of payment, and concert listings. The information drawn from these texts further structures and clarifies our interaction with the ticket seller.

Texts form part of what Hollan, Hutchins, and Kirsh (2000, p. 181) call a "cognitive architecture," a configuration of resources and relationships that provide cognitive assistance to those who carry out work in the environment where the architecture is located. A cognitive architecture consists of supports for physical and cognitive work, resources that extend and coordinate the work of individuals. For example, technologies like personal computers and personal digital assistants extend a person's access to information. Forms help users transform their knowledge and observations into familiar information.

Cognitive architectures of text and technology can be quite broad, mediating the work of an entire organization. The architecture can also be local, mediating the work of an individual at his or her desk. Some cognitive architectures are

1

stable in that they are built up over time. Others are emergent in that they accommodate activities that require an ad hoc arrangement of resources.

As work environments become more richly laminated with texts and information technologies, what burdens are placed on professionals who must learn to contribute to the discursive activities they mediate? This question forms the basis of the inquiry running throughout the book. It is a line of inquiry that stems from a historical observation that texts have become the heart of broadly-social, organized activities. In spite of the broad institutional roles texts play, writing is still considered a highly individualized activity. This perception is further reinforced by writing technologies (e.g., the *personal* computer), but often overlooked in organizational practices such as writing review, where texts "graduate" from individual to organizational status. The point that remains unclear is how the text-mediated structure of an organization emerges in texts and how newcomers learn to recognize and produce it.

Many professionals must become effective communicators in order to participate in text-rich and technology-rich work environments. They must learn to use and produce the texts that mediate organizational activities. As the work of many fields becomes increasingly mediated by information technology, more responsibility falls to professionals in those fields to contribute to the textual architecture that mediates that work. This move toward greater textuality has proven problematic, because it requires that the work of many different professions be partly redefined as communication work, even though professionals in those fields (e.g., engineering) do not see themselves as writers. Some professions are beginning to recognize the importance that text plays in structuring their work, but are slow to provide structured opportunities for professionals to become better writers. The paradoxical relationship between the recognized need for training in writing and the often remarkably poor execution of writing review practices (see Bernhardt, 2003), underscores the need to examine the situation and to evaluate our ability to respond. If we step back and examine why many professions have become text-oriented, we can better understand the problems associated with preparing professionals to use and contribute to this textual architecture. When we can see the variety of relationships supported by texts, we will be better able to envision new and better ways to promote enculturation through writing review.

THE NEED FOR TEXTUAL MEDIATION

In 1992, Robert Reich observed a change in the American workforce as it moved away from a model of problem solving to one of problem solving *and* problem creation. In the problem-solving model, the dominant mode of production was manufacturing and craftsmanship. Companies identified consumer needs and met them. Profitability was tied to a company's ability to identify consumer need and to its capacity for satisfying that need. In the latter part of the

20th century, this business model shifted away from satisfying a narrow range of customer needs to addressing a more diverse range of needs. More importantly, the business model shifted away from satisfying *current* customer needs to creating new customer needs.

The shift in labor practices is important as a backdrop for discussing a change in the kind of labor that is valued in this new economy. Instead of privileging craft-based knowledge, the modern economy privileges knowledge related to the articulation and communication of customer needs, as well as that related to the coordination of organizational efforts to meet those needs. The knowledge and ability to fashion and articulate new consumer needs is as valued, if not more so, as knowledge associated with the ability to satisfy those demands. Yet as Reich points out, knowledge is difficult to retain. As people leave companies, they take their knowledge with them, a problem that has led to renewed interest in the power of writing and text to commodify knowledge, to give it a physical, shareable form. For this reason, among others, the 20th century saw the rise of a new kind of professional, one that Reich calls the "symbol analyst," who "[simplifies] reality into abstract images that can be rearranged, juggled, experimented with, communicated to other specialists, and then, eventually, transformed back into reality" (1992, p. 178). In other words, many professionals have become writers.

Modern workplaces are environments that have, over time, become suffused with texts that mediate the work of colleagues within a division, across divisions, and across organizations. One explanation for the prevalence of texts and their increasingly prominent roles is the contribution they make to the practice of systematic management (see Douglas, 1986; Gee, Hull, and Lankshear, 1996; Yates, 1993). Texts allow greater control over, and organization of, resources.

A related benefit of text is that it allows knowledge to be distributed. Using texts, people can work independently and apply information from texts to a variety of work activities. While allowing some degree of freedom, texts also constrain work by creating and reinforcing conventional uses of information, which in turn reinforce particular working relationships among colleagues (see Henderson, 1991; Winsor, 1996, 2001). For example, a text may contain specifications for a product design, including CAD (computer aided design) drawings that are only comprehensible and changeable by people with knowledge of CAD. Texts with CAD create a necessary information-sharing relationship between a group of users and people who can read and change CAD drawings. However, not all work relationships are routine enough to be supported by texts with fixed form. Some relationships emerge as situations warrant, and the texts that mediate those relationships serve an entirely different and somewhat unpredictable purpose.

Not surprisingly, organizations generate voluminous amounts of text for a variety of specialized purposes. In common practice, these texts become connected to routine work activities and emerge as genres. Genres splinter and become more specialized, acquiring supplemental texts that support ancillary work activities. Together, these sets of genres (Yates and Orlikowski, 1994, 2002) mediate more complex, coordination-dependent work activities. One important implication is that writing is a way that professionals participate in an organization's discursive activity.

Organizational work practices are abstractions that describe the work of individuals whose efforts are coordinated, in part, by the texts they all produce and share. It is a fact of many professions that people work with others more often than they work in isolation. They work for complex organizations that carry out tasks that are impossible for a single person to do alone. For example, monitoring industry compliance with air quality standards is far too complex for a single environmental engineer. Likewise, managing the public relations and the donor relations activities for a large private university is more likely to be the work of a group than a single person. More often than not, these collective work practices are mediated by expansive constellations of texts (see Devitt, 1991).

The coordination required to carry out these complex activities implies cooperation and activity that extends beyond what a single person does at his or her desk. Complex work activities require people to offload cognitive effort to other people, texts, and technologies in the environments where they work. Work that is offloaded to texts, inputted to computer files, and shared with colleagues, is transformed and structured such that it can be used in pursuit of other related activities. Hutchins' (1995) example of the migration of information across representational states shows how observations of landmarks are transformed into bearings, which are recorded as numerals that can be transferred to a nautical chart. Similar transformations happen in other organizations as information passes through different technological interfaces. The texts and technologies of text enable the coordination out of which collective action arises.

Texts help structure work activity in a number of ways. The first is that the design of a text, especially one based on organizational genres, implies a social contract between writers and readers. A text may have formatting that divides information into labeled sections that define both the kind of information required and the relationships between pieces of information (Bazerman, 2000). Blank fields can indicate what kind of information should be collected and how that information should be represented (e.g., the conventions for reporting traffic scene information on accident reports). Texts can contain a wealth of information in structure alone. Their design can turn the complex task(s) that they mediate into simple tasks that people are exceedingly good at (e.g., filling in blanks, following directions, recognizing patterns). Texts with these fixed, designed forms embody the experiences and motivations of those who designed them. By learning to use these texts, one learns the behaviors and social responsibilities that come with participating in a work activity supported by such texts (see Latour, 1995). Still, knowledge of how to use a text is not wholly embedded in the design.

Texts are also embedded in rule-governed social settings, and within these settings, texts are embedded in technological contexts. Readers and writers access their texts through a variety of technological interfaces (e.g., paper, databases, word processors) that portray the texts in various states of completion, approval, comprehensiveness, and authority. Consider the difference between seeing paragraphs of text written in a personal e-mail versus the same paragraphs printed on company letterhead. In the former medium, the paragraphs may appear more tentative and open for discussion. In the latter, the paragraphs may appear more fixed and final. Uses of those texts are shaped as much by their content as by the social and technological contexts in which readers encounter them. Each reader has a responsibility to understand the social contexts in which texts are used and the technological contexts through which texts are accessed. Only with this information can readers decide on the best way to contribute to these activities discursively.

FIXED AND FLUID INFORMATION
IN TEXTS

Describing the impact of technology on writing and information, David Levy notes that technology has ensured a certain degree of fixity and fluidity in information (2001, p. 38). While some media theorists suggest that modern information technology is leading to a postmodern condition of unbound, acontextual information (see Bolter, 2001), observations of information use in various settings reminds us that it is always tied to very concrete activities (Brown and Duguid, 2000; Sellen and Harper, 2002) that require fixed information. Yet even routine activities defy expectations. Routine activities are also situated and often require information to be fluid and adaptable (Suchman, 1987).

The desire for fixed and fluid information has resulted in parallel trends of technology development that help reinforce our perceptions of information as fixed or fluid. Throughout the 19th and 20th centuries, people recognized the importance of information and the effect of information (or lack of) on work practice. Driven by a need to manage increasingly complex work activities, companies became early adopters of technologies like copy machines, typewriters, carbon paper, and filing cabinets (see Yates, 1993, pp. 21-64), all of which helped give knowledge a representational form. The resulting fixed nature of information helped mediate work relationships by regularizing them, making them systematic, as notable in the control of assembly-line work (Gee, Hull, and Lankshear, 1996), the management of railroads (Yates, 1993, pp. 101-158), and the practice of providing medical care (Schryer and Spoel, 2005).

The desire for fixed information also coincided with a desire for more fluid information. While a typewriter may have made it possible to record information, set policies and standard procedures, the typewriter also made it possible to change those texts and redistribute the results more easily. Modern information technologies, like personal digital assistants and cellular phones, also make information fluid and changeable to accommodate situation-specific, ad hoc work practices (see Churchill and Munro, 2001; Gillette, 2001) and to accommodate work practices that rely on continually updated information (see Sellen and Harper, 2002, pp. 78-105).

Another way to summarize the difference between fixed and fluid information is in the kind of coordination they facilitate. Fixed information encourages coordination across an organization by holding individuals to standards set forth in a corpus of texts acting as an organization's collective knowledge (Devitt, 1991). Yet all organizational activity is comprised of much smaller, more local acts of coordination—people working with each other and building coordination through interaction (Medway, 1996). These situated work practices rely on fluid information.

Two observations follow from this discussion. The first is that the technologies we surround ourselves with make information fixed and fluid in ways that accommodate specific interactions between users. Learning to produce texts in an organizational context requires writers to recognize the need for fixed and fluid information. Based on that information, writers must choose representational technologies that afford the production of such information while still allowing them to fulfill personal motivations for writing. The second observation is that many work relationships require information to be fixed and fluid. Because of the nature of the work relationship, only information of a certain type can provide beneficial mediation.

Writing review is a work practice that illustrates the complexity of text use. At once, writing review is an organizationally sanctioned activity in which reviewers assess a text's appropriateness as a fixed information object. At the same time, the writing review is a point of enculturation. The reviewer is a more experienced peer who must work with the writer to develop an appropriate textual contribution. In this sense, the text is a fluid information object, a contribution that is under development.

A cognitive architecture that supports the enculturation of professionals to their text-rich environments will require the presence of tools for representing texts as fixed (to show the relationship to the work of the organization) and fluid (to show a text's development as part of a writer's literate participation). In writing review, the most common tool, paper, does not show texts as fluid information objects, thus cutting off opportunities for effective cooperation between writers and reviewers. The problem is compounded by the fact that reviewers do not see their role as pedagogical. Furthermore, writing reviews tend to occur late in a writing cycle, when writers are more inclined to think that their texts are finished. In practice and in appearance, reviewed texts appear to merit evaluation as fixed information objects, even if the texts reflect writers' difficulty in constructing appropriate literate contributions.

APPROPRIATE TECHNOLOGICAL SUPPORT
FOR REVISION AND REVIEW

Initially, learning to write requires guidance from more experienced practitioners who know how texts contribute to the coordination of organizational work practices. One of the more common methods for providing this guidance is writing review, in which supervisors, subject matter experts, and even peers read a text with the dual aim of assessing its "fit" as a fixed information resource (Paradis, Dobrin, and Miller, 1985, p. 293) and assisting writers in developing an awareness of organizational needs that translate into specific writing practices. To support these two goals, the writers and reviewers must treat reviewed texts as fixed manifestations of organizational genres that will successfully or unsuccessfully meet user expectations. A reviewer can best fulfill these supervisory responsibilities when treating the text as an object of fixed information.

The review participants must also treat the text as an object that represents a stage in a writing process, where text is under negotiation and incomplete. One aim of writing review is for writers and reviewers to work cooperatively on a text so that the writer learns by acting with a more experienced practitioner. The reviewer can best serve this pedagogical role when treating the reviewed text as a representation of a stage in an ongoing writing process.

There are two problems in thinking about the text as both a fixed and a fluid information object. The first is that supervisory and pedagogical reviewer roles are built around contrasting motives. Where the supervisor's motive might be to take responsibility for a text and to alter it to fit organizational needs, a reviewer providing pedagogical assistance must be willing to work with what the writer is trying to accomplish. Many reviewers will find it difficult to move between these motives because few are trained as professional writers, and fewer still are trained to offer any kind of writing instruction (Schriver, 1989).

The second and more serious problem is a lack of an appropriate organizational and technological structure to support review with both aims. One's ability to perform a task is based in part on having the right environment in which to perform it (Hutchins, 1995, p. 169). Given how quickly the work of many professions is being redefined as communication-related, it is not surprising that some organizations lack an appropriate structure to support training in writing. It is clear, however, that the arrangement of resources and conventional practice of writing review can have an influential effect on the kinds or writer/reviewer relationships that can form.

In a writing review, participants will ideally examine the text from the perspectives of organizational need and writer intent. These perspectives must be brought into conversation so that writers can make connections between their writing and the work of the organization at large, between knowing what they want to say and knowing what the organization needs them to say. However, a number of other factors make it difficult for reviewers and writers to engage in an equitable discussion of a text's fixed and fluid qualities. For one, writers and reviewers often lack enough common ground to coordinate the organizational and practice-oriented perspectives. The writers often lack the reviewers' enculturated experience, making it difficult for them to envision the relevant organizational needs for a text. For the reviewers, writing for the organization is a process that has become so natural that it is generally tacit (Polanyi, 1974; Ryle, 1949). As a result, reviewers spent little time talking about writing practices and more time fiddling with sentence level details and idiosyncrasies of form (van der Geest and van Gemert, 1997, pp. 437-441). This kind of review is further encouraged by common review practices, such as writers waiting to initiate review until they feel their texts are finished, rather than submitting rough drafts that might reveal information about writing process. An argument developed in this book is that this kind of review can arrest a writer's ability to participate in a discourse community organized around textual contributions.

Reviews often occur between participants who do not consider themselves writers, at a point in the writing process when writers consider their texts finished. Reviews occur in settings that are isolated from the complex organizational work activities supported by the text(s) reviewed. Reviews are conducted in technological contexts that contain only static images of a writer's composing practices. Under these conditions, it will be easier to critique texts as fixed information objects, because that is how they appear, and that is how the reviewer/writer relationship is operationally defined as a routine practice.

As a point of contrast, consider that a writing classroom has an altogether different configuration of resources that does support a teacher/student relationship focused on a discussion of writing process. At least part of the time, writers compose in class. Teachers see multiple drafts. Review is a frequent and iterative practice, and there is no dominant set of organizational constraints that drive a student's writing process. The ideal role for reviewers is instructional. In fact, Katz (1998b) has suggested "the supervisor's role as reviewer or editor may be one of the most significant mechanisms for *teaching* [emphasis added] newcomers how to write appropriately in the organization" (p. 170).

While the motivation for providing instructional support may exist, many reviewers lack appropriate support for providing instruction. A lack of access to the writer at the point of composition is one such constraint. With appropriate support, however, reviewers may be better able to offer pedagogical insight on work that newcomers produce. Classroom resources are set up to facilitate cooperative work and to present texts in their fluid, transitional forms. Pieces of a similar cognitive architecture are often conspicuously absent in many organizational settings. One noticeable manifestation of this problem is in the technological support for writers and reviewers.

By changing the arrangement and availability of resources that support review, it is possible to create different opportunities for interaction between writers and reviewers. Would writing review in organizations be different if the available resources were reconfigured to encourage cooperation, to provide a picture of text in a more fluid form? How would the character of review be different if the means for conducting it more directly accommodated the dual motives of improving texts and improving writing?

This book considers the answers to the above questions by offering an analysis of writers and the different cognitive architectures in which they work toward enculturation. The book addresses the question of how writers become enculturated to their writing-intensive work duties through writing review, a practice that differs between organizations because of the nature of resources available to support it. The book also considers the role that text and the technologies of text play in supporting and encouraging particular writer/reviewer relationships and specific writing review practices. Writing review is a practice in which newcomers learn about the various demands on their texts, and it is also a site at which those demands are played out. By studying how the roles between writers and reviewers are sustained by, and dependent on, the local cognitive architectures of review, we will come away with a model for thinking about the influence of information technology on review and with a model for planning new technologies.

To facilitate this analytic comparison, this book compares the outcomes of two different configurations of technology to support writing review in two different kinds of organizations. The analysis focuses on the importance of an adequate cognitive architecture to support relationships between writers and reviewers that lead to a better articulation of how texts and organizational activity are co-constituted. The book also offers a methodology for conducting research on technological mediation that derives from examinations of local writing review practices.

This book is built around these hypotheses.

- In organizations where there is an appropriate and accommodating cognitive architecture—one that supports cooperative discussion of writing process and organizational demands—there will be less need for mediational changes.
- In organizations where this architecture is not in place, where technologies reinforce the invisibility of writing, changes to the technological configuration of writing review space will help create conditions for enculturation.

Discussion of these issues will allow us to understand what it takes for professionals to learn to participate in the literate activities of complex organizations that are increasingly text-dependent. We will also be able to discuss, more directly, the role of information technology as it pertains to enculturation.

CHAPTER OUTLINE

Together with Technology is a book about the mediation provided by information technology in writing review. It is a book that compares how people in writing professions and those not typically associated with writing learn to become practicing writers. The book also considers what can be learned about the cognitive architectures that support writing review. How do both kinds of organizations restructure writing review practices when the technologies mediating that practice are changed? Where this book differs from other treatments of writing review and enculturation is that it examines the social and mediating role of technology.

By reading this book you will come away with an understanding of:

- How text and other information technologies contribute to the creation and maintenance of local cognitive architectures.
- Why enculturation and enculturation support for professionals who write is necessarily tied to an analysis of the technology.
- How technological mediation helps create opportunities for people to interact with each other and with existing resources to better facilitate enculturation.
- How observations of these writing review practices can inform the development of information technologies to support writing review.

Chapter 1 covers the evolving role of text and textual technologies in modern organizations by tying in studies of genre and systematic management to theories of distributed cognition. The central argument is that texts of all stripes and technological forms directly contribute to organizational coordination and thus play prominent roles in the course of daily work activities.

Chapter 2 explores the practice of writing review in more depth, considering the organizational functions that it serves. The chapter covers the practices by which writing reviews are typically conducted, as well as two goals for writing review that are based on Susan Kleimann's (1993) work. The first goal is to bring the text into coordination with the needs of the organization. The second goal is to assist writers in a revision of their work, both to improve the text and to help writers see how to contribute to the organization via writing. Discussion of these issues draws on numerous studies of writing review that show how the practice itself is a site of enculturation where reviewers scaffold writers' participation in organizational networks of activity. Coordination is shown to be an essential element of enculturation, one that requires professionals to develop an understanding of how to interact with other people, resources, and texts.

Chapter 3 narrows the discussion by looking more directly at the local cognitive architectures of people and material resources that typically support writing review. Drawing on information about enculturation, this chapter covers how writers and reviewers seek coordination and interactively engage in coordination-building activities. The ability to achieve coordination is constrained and afforded by technology and other available resources. The chapter then moves on to technologies and resources that are typically available during writing review, where it is suggested why some types of coordination needed to carry out the dual motives of writing review are more difficult to achieve with those technological resources. Textual replay is introduced as a technology that offers a new kind of mediation to facilitate coordination that could result in learning.

Chapter 4 sets up the study reported in the book and provides details about the analysis upon which the discussion of the book is based. The method for analyzing changes in writing review practices is derived from work by Spinuzzi (2003). This approach involves breaking down revision and review into the general aims of those practices (e.g., "improve the writer's skills"), the actions that constitute those activities (e.g., "propose revisions," "discuss options"), and the operations by which those actions are carried out (e.g., "questioning," "rephrasing"). The impact of technological mediation will be observed as differences in the increased or decreased presence of particular writing review activities and in the different ways that those activities are operationalized.

This chapter also provides information about the organizational sites of study (city desk at a newspaper, environmental engineering agency, university donor relations office, university media relations office). For each organization, the character, motivation, and support for writing review are topics of discussion.

Chapter 5 summarizes the differences between the writing review sessions that were mediated by text only and those that were mediated by a combination of text and textual replay. The purpose of the chapter is to point to the ways in which writers and reviewers at all of the organizational sites interacted similarly in the text mediated reviews compared to their actions in writing review mediated by text and textual replay. By comparing text mediation to textual replay + text mediation, readers can speculate how consistent differences in review practices could be attributed to features of the texts, textual replays, and to the manner in which both were used during the reviews.

Organizations like the newspaper and the university media relations offices were practice-oriented in that the aim of the reviews was to support the improvement of writing practices. Organizations like the environmental engineering agency and the university donor relations office were artifact-oriented in that the focus of the review sessions was on coordinating the writer's text (the knowledge artifact) with other texts in the organization and with the larger overarching goals of the organization. Chapters 6 and 7 focus more specifically on the writing review practices of the practice-oriented and artifact-oriented organizations, respectively. The purpose of these chapters is to draw a distinction between the two types of organizations distinguished by the character of the existing cognitive architecture for supporting writing review.

These chapters also contain a discussion about how the review practices in practice-oriented and artifact-oriented organizations differed and how the review participants appeared to make use of the opportunities for interaction presented by the text and textual replay. In many cases, the textual replay afforded different kinds of interaction that allowed the writers and reviewers to achieve levels of coordination that were not present in the writing reviews mediated by text alone.

Chapter 8 concludes the book by looking at the ways the textual replay was used in the writing reviews across the different organizations. These observations are used as evidence for theorizing the development of a textual replay technology that will support the multiple purposes of writing review more directly. The chapter concludes with a discussion of what worked well and poorly about textual replay and with a way to turn these observations into design suggestions for building a textual replay technology that is better suited to reviews across organizations.

More generally, Chapter 8 is a discussion of how the research reported in this book points to the need for studying local text-mediated practices as the basis for theorizing and developing new information technology for a variety of organizational practices, not just writing review. Scholars of technical and professional communication are ideally suited for this kind of research.

CHAPTER 1

Texts and Knowledge Work

Professional practices in many fields are increasingly tied to writing and communication. Such changes are evident in fields that have not typically been associated with writing (e.g., engineers, paramedics, programmers). A number of factors contribute to this overall change, chiefly the continued development and adoption of information technology, as well as more general economic shifts from production and manufacturing, and to information brokering.

One result of this general shift toward textuality is that the designation "writer" is more broadly applied across a greater range of disciplines, whose members are not necessarily trained as writers or critically aware of the writing that they do. Writing ability and awareness of the audiences and tasks supported by texts comes from interaction with the information technologies by which these texts are generated, as well as from participation in the text-supported interactions encouraged by these technologies. In many cases, the processes by which people learn to write have been shaped by the textual and technological networks where they write. Writers and reviewers alike may be largely unaware of how texts and information technologies shape the writers' interactions with their texts, their interactions with reviewers, their interactions with colleagues (distributed, physically and temporally), and their awareness of the work their texts do. Writers may be unaware of the extent to which their texts build an organization in both a supportive and formative way. Moreover, the sheer number and importance of texts underscores the importance of structured managerial/pedagogical practices like writing review. Despite good intentions, however, writing review often struggles to provide the clarity of purpose and process that helps writers develop their craft. In part, we can attribute the problem to the complexity of the task and to the level of technological support (the latter of which will be the subject of Chapter 3).

One central complicating factor in writing review is that texts have become connected to the ontological status of organizations in very significant ways, making it difficult for writing review to be about a single text composed by a single writer, because such a perspective falsely atomizes the text and the process by which it is created. In 1986, Stephen Doheny-Farina noted a "reciprocal relationship between writing and the development of an organization" (p. 180). He suggested that the act of writing has a powerful formative effect on the structure and operation of organizations. Writers create supportive social relationships and change the structure of existing relationships. At the same time, the act of writing is just as constrained by existing organizational structure as writing review. We will better understand the work of writing review when we examine how texts contribute to this organizational structure and how this structure shapes the ways writers learn to produce it. The brief historical sketch that follows will show how changes in economic history have set a stage for vast and pervasive reliance on texts that serve complex cognitive and sociological functions. Following this historical background will be a discussion of the impact on what we commonly perceive to be the functions of texts and the work environments that they foster.

TEXTS IN EMERGING ORGANIZATIONAL CULTURES

The importance of text can be partially contextualized by looking at concurrent historical developments in ways to manage labor, promote effective coordination, formalize knowledge and expertise, and manage information resources. These practices are important motivations in scientific management (Taylor, 1911/1967) and systematic management (see Douglas, 1986; Yates, 1993) alike.

As early as the mid 19th century, businesses that had relied on the labor of skilled artisans had begun to consider ways to make the artistry of that work more tangible, so that the knowledge could be preserved and passed on to others. This desire contributed to work models where "both the acquisition and the practice of occupational skills were . . . reduced to a framework of ordered, written rules which could form the basis of a complex yet rational, hierarchical, and above all stable economic order" (Vincent, 1993, p. 104). In such "old capitalism" models, employees were "hired from the neck down [and] had only to follow directions and mechanically carry out a rather meaningless piece of process that they did not need to understand as a whole" (Gee, Hull, and Lankshear, 1996, p. 26). Employees lacked a holistic knowledge of the work processes to which they contributed, knowing instead only their circumscribed pieces of those processes.

In such settings, managers were paid to be aware of factors that would improve efficiency and effectiveness. These motivations prompted like-minded engineers to consider ways that labor could be described scientifically, with the assistance of time and motion studies that promised to replace inefficient "rule-of-thumb" knowledge with scientific observations and articulations of work practices.

Taylor (1911/1967) proposed, "every single act of every workman can be reduced to a science" (p. 64), and to the managers should fall the responsibility of

> gathering together all of the traditional knowledge which in the past [had] been possessed by the workmen, and then . . . classifying, tabulating, and reducing this knowledge to rules, laws, and formulae which are immensely helpful to the workmen in doing their daily work (p. 36).

Taylor's opinion was that workers would be more efficient with their energy focused on smaller, well-defined tasks. Consequently, Taylor's method of management required managers to develop ways to articulate work procedures and to distribute this information. The division of labor into smaller tasks and the distribution of this effort over a larger workforce resulted in people working jointly, but independently, on a single activity. The distribution of effort improved production while introducing a problem of coordination. Effective work required coordination both within a population of people performing the same task (vertical coordination), but also among employees working on different, but complementary tasks (horizontal coordination). Strict job descriptions, procedures documents, company rules, and other texts sought to provide the coordination of effort lost through distribution.

Taylor's time and motion studies readily led to the articulation of precise, timed movements that formed the basis of these emerging organization-oriented texts. However, additional texts were needed to coordinate the work of individuals. Taylor's monograph does not much consider horizontal coordination, but the ideas and assumptions behind scientific management are entirely applicable. The role of texts in supporting horizontal coordination is more directly addressed in texts concerned with systematic management (of which scientific management is considered a variant (Yates, 1993, p. 10)).

In systematic management, coordination is mandated from the top down. Upper level management decides how to organize the collective work of individuals. They pass down texts serving that effect. Managers also engage in the monitoring and evaluation of work at lower levels (Yates, 1993, p. 10). Both activities require texts for specifying work practices, articulating team goals, communicating changes to employees, and reporting information to management. Whereas Taylor's interest in such texts was in quantifying an "honest day's labor" and creating justification for wages and hiring/firing decisions, in systematic management the texts were used to create organizational structure that supported systemic work practices.

In both systems of management, texts came to serve important and complex functions. One was that *texts expressed knowledge and experience in a common and accessible representational form* (e.g., rules, laws, and formulae). The language of science and engineering provided a ready lexicon for explaining knowledge that had been considered more "natural" and "tacit," existing in the hands and eyes of the practitioners (see Polanyi, 1972, 1983; Ryle, 1949). The extent to which texts actually articulate tacit knowledge is a matter of considerable debate; nevertheless, there is greater consensus that texts provide at least a tangible and shareable representation of knowledge and experience, which allows information to spread horizontally and vertically in an organization.

A second function for texts is training. *Texts record scientific observations and make the recorded actions comprehensible to those learning them.* These pedagogical needs encouraged the development of training genres, starting with Taylor's training cards and continuing with newer genres of training manuals, posters, and all manner of texts associated with training courses and calibration events. These training materials have also become effective means of shaping the work of employees (see Gee, Hull, and Lankshear, 1996, pp. 73-103).

The third function is that *texts support both the distribution and coordination of labor.* A text that specifies the goals and procedures of a task enables the user to work without continual supervision, because people who learn their trades in the same way, using the same texts, effectively self-coordinate. The associated downside is that some texts can over-determine work practices that are naturally more ad hoc and situated than the guiding texts suggest. Texts that acquire organizational authority and which become connected to hiring, firing, and advancement can easily constrain the better judgment of employees who recognize a need to deviate from approved procedures but do not for fear of reprisal (e.g., see Gee, Hull, and Lankshear, 1996, p. 123).

The same influence survives today both in the way that texts shape organizational action and in the ways that genres crystallize those actions (Miller, 1984), an effect multiplied many times over to produce whole systems of interrelated, information-sharing relationships between people, technologies, and texts. These texts enable what Yates (1993) calls "control through communication," which, in its worst forms, creates uniformity and conformity with stultifying effects on employees who are required to submit to the authority of the texts they are given. Such practices are roundly and rightly criticized (Douglas, 1986; Gee, Hull, and Lankshear, 1996; Geisler, 2001; Smith, 1984), because they contribute to a perceived "de-skilling" of individual labor, to the creation of new literacy burdens for participation, and to the shifting of work safety responsibility to employees who don't "follow the rules" (Sauer, 1998).

Although scientific and systematic management are related, they aim to control different kinds of labor. The work Taylor describes is almost exclusively physical (e.g., sizing wheel bearings, brick laying, and hauling pig iron). In her analysis, Yates, too, describes the importance of managing physical labor, but expands her analysis to include information-centered labor, such as managing work processes and coordinating train schedules. In the latter, some labor is redirected to the production and maintenance of text, which constitutes the structure in which that work takes place. These theories reflect a shifting economic picture that further explains the thorough integration of text into the work of organizations.

OLD CAPITALISM AND NEW

The principles of early systematic management were based on a model of work that primarily utilized physical labor. This economic model has undergone significant change as the world-economic picture has changed to favor work that is more information-driven. The "old capitalism" was

> based on the mass production of (relatively uniform) goods by large, hierarchically structured corporations serving a commodities-starved, but progressively richer post-World War II population in the developed world (Gee, Hull, and Lankshear, 1996, p. 26).

By contrast, "new capitalism" is based on the design, production, and marketing of "high quality" goods and services for new saturated markets (1996, p. 26). In the new capitalism, profitability has switched from mass production of goods to fill established needs, to the production of those needs and the design of solutions for them. That is, production and profitability have become more closely tied to the management of information and knowledge required for identifying customer need and designing solutions. This kind of knowledge is considerably more difficult to describe scientifically.

This shift in labor practices does not diminish the importance of text so much as it redefines its organizational work. Texts have gone from being artifacts that support the control of manual labor to being the products of labor in an information economy. They have become the metaphorical bricks and mortar that support organizational work practices that generate those products.

Writing about this economic evolution, Robert Reich (2003) noted that since the 1960's, the number of jobs in manufacturing has diminished from a point where they accounted for nearly a third of all jobs in the United States, to a point now where they account for only about a sixth. The jobs are not simply moving overseas; they appear to be vanishing altogether, largely due to the way that we define "manufacturing" and the labor that it entails. Since the 1960s, we have experienced a lateral expansion of the category of "manufacturing." Many of the manufacturing dollars associated with a given product often come back to the United States in the form of payment to a growing cadre of designers, engineers, marketers, lawyers and managers, all of whom participate in the manufacturing process by producing and managing information.

Economic success is often linked to effective design, innovation, customer research, marketing, legal protection, product distribution and process management, all of which are information-based activities. Within many professional practices associated with a manufactured product, the product is conceived of and manipulated as symbolic content: a design idea, customer preferences, legal statutes, and manufacturing processes. The texts that contain this information both mediate the production process and create grounds on which these professionals coordinate their work.

There are two important implications in Reich's observations. The first is that the redefinition of manufacturing work points to the incredible diversity of professional labor that is coordinated (both cognitively and socially) in the fulfillment of a generic "manufacturing" process. Second, Reich hints at the importance of information and texts as agents that facilitate this coordination.

These professionals, whose work is largely information-based, constitute a professional class that Reich (1992) has dubbed "symbol analysts." The symbol analysts

> solve, identify, and broker problems by manipulating symbols. They simplify reality into abstract images that can be rearranged, juggled, experimented with, communicated to other specialists, and then, eventually, transformed back into reality (1992, p. 178).

The range of professions that Reich defines as symbol analytic is diverse, the common thread being that professionals in those fields are writers in so far as their work is shaped by their ability to create and manipulate symbolic content. Symbol analysts produce text and interact with other symbol analysts via text. As a result, texts have shifted to the center of many organizational practices, becoming common places upon which work is based and around which it is organized.

In an economy based on the production and use of symbols, texts acquire importance and stature above that described in scientific and systematic management. Professionals use texts to structure their own work as well as their work-related interactions with colleagues. Texts have become so ubiquitous and integrated to professional practices that they are inseparable from the work professionals may consider to be their primary occupation. Writing can no longer be separated from design, from research, from testing, or from a host of other professional duties. The reason is that texts such as schematics, data tables, and test reports provide necessary structure to information that must be shared and accessed in very circumscribed ways. Certainly, texts mediate the work of individuals, but the many ways that textual form and content have become formalized point to their indispensability as tools of social organization and coordination.

These historical explanations illustrate the complex social and cognitive roles that texts play in structuring professional labor in organizations. But a closer consideration of the dynamics by which texts contribute to this structure will allow us to better understand the ideal objectives of writing review in professional settings that are rich with texts. Texts provide versatile mediation for individual and group cognitive activity while creating fixed and fluid information sharing relationships that literally and figuratively create organizational structure.

THE COGNITIVE, SOCIAL, AND ORGANIZATIONAL
ROLES OF TEXT

As should be clear from the discussion in the previous section, texts are complex socio-cognitive artifacts whose importance extends well beyond the mediation of individual activities. In some ways, texts take on lives of their own and become imbued with cognitive and social qualities that make them difficult to write. In addition, we must also consider that texts combine to form whole ecologies of information resources (see Spinuzzi, 2003) that structure writing and review even while creating new kinds of agency for writers and reviewers.

Learning to write requires a person to learn the work that his or her text will do. With regard to writing in an organizational setting, we can argue, as Latour (1986) does, that texts fix information (in form, place, time) while also making it more fluid and adaptable to multiple, simultaneous uses (see also Levy, 1994, 2001). Fixed information facilitates record keeping and the creation of a corpus of texts that informs and collectively structures the work of individuals. Fluid information facilitates new kinds of agency at the level of individuals. It does so by keeping information abstract and uncommitted to a specific application. Individuals can use this information ad hoc, in service of situated information needs, and in support of local efforts of coordination. In this way, texts structure the work of individuals by fixing a context of work, but also by leaving the local enactment of work more flexible. Writing review and writer training must create a pedagogical frame that accounts for this full range of complex uses. Texts.

- fix information in a stable form;
- promote learning and training;
- support adaptive uses of information;
- promote the development of organizational structure;
- comprise part of an organization-wide cognitive architecture.

Texts to Fix Information

One primary function served by texts is that they preserve information. Unlike our memories, texts create high-fidelity and more durable records of information. Texts are immutable (Latour, 1986, p. 21) meaning that their content resists change, no matter how often it is copied and shared. In addition to fixing information, texts also fix lexicons and modes of expression. With the assistance of information technologies, texts can be reproduced and distributed to the far reaches of an organization, creating stability to the extent that organizational activities will all refer to a common set of uniformly-expressed procedures, rules, conventions, and habits of mind (see Levy, 1994, p. 25).

Texts preserve formal representations of knowledge and ideas, and in doing so carry forward some of the context in which those ideas were formed (see

Bazerman, Little, and Chavkin, 2003). This stability arises from a text's immutability, but also from its permanence. Very simply, once ideas are written down, copied, and distributed, they are much more difficult to eliminate (Goody and Watt, 1968, p. 66). Unlike memories, texts are less easily forgotten, especially with the assistance of archives and archiving technologies. Collectively, texts become part of tangible organizational memory, a physical manifestation of organizational knowledge and action (Devitt, 1991, pp. 336-337, 351).

Texts also do more than fix content. They also fix the ways information can be interpreted and used. In Hutchins' (1997) words, texts "mediate" activity in that they provide a clarifying structure that is not inherent in the task accomplished (p. 338). Examples would include emissions regulations that help engineers recognize a business's improper equipment configuration, as well as donor lists (with previous donation information) to help donor relations officers determine how to address donors in solicitation letters. These texts, and others like them, are public, produced in large quantities, and shared throughout organizations, ensuring mediation that extends throughout an organization.

For texts to help fix interpretation, they must carry forward some information about context that writers would be challenged to express in words alone. Bazerman et al. (2003) suggest that such contextual information is carried forward as recognizable genre traits, regularities in content and modes of expression that indicate a text's genealogical connection to other genres (p. 474). Literally, the words and modes of expression a writer chooses reveal some information about valued ways of thinking and acting. This argument is connected to an earlier one proposed by Goody and Watt (1968, pp. 53-54) who argued that with text, writers could arrange information visually (e.g., the stacked visual presentation of a logical syllogism) in ways that facilitated acts of logical interpretation.

The clues and supports for interpretation are frequently embedded in the design of the texts. Structural inventions like punctuation, page layout, and spacing all contribute to a reader's ability to form interpretations of content within a given context (see Kostelnick and Roberts, 1998; Olson, 1995, pp. 91-114; Schriver, 1997). Some interpretive guidance could be conveyed by choices of paper, font, and color. More often, writers telegraph intended uses of information by choosing to express it in a given structural form. For instance, parallel arrangements indicate simultaneous actions; hierarchical arrangements appear to order tasks by importance; taxonomic arrangements group related tasks and subtasks; and sequential arrangements specify an order of actions. Hutchins calls these designed elements "meta-mediational," structures that are designed to help readers understand how to interpret the content (1997, p. 340).

A related advantage to fixing interpretation is that by doing so, individuals are nudged into coordination with others who interpret their work in similar and/or complementary ways. On one level, tasks relying on common texts operate from the same information. Also present in those texts is some indication of how one is expected to use the information, i.e., "instructions" that are present in texts as recognizable genred characteristics. Format choices and other visual structures reflect the insights of designers who understood how information-processing activities coordinate with others in a given task.

Meta-mediational structures create fixed ways of interpreting information for use in service of a given task. For example, a veterinarian who is seeing a patient must create a list of potential causes for observed conditions. To assist in the diagnosis, the veterinarian may consult a medical reference, which contains visual and verbal descriptions of symptoms related to likely conditions. The visual and verbal descriptions are one level of mediation for structuring and clarifying observations the veterinarian may make during a physical exam. The medical reference provides another level of mediation by structuring diagnostic information into flow charts and fishbone diagrams, leading the users through a series of yes/no questions that point to likely causes. The visual aids represent the accumulated knowledge passed on by veterinarians about how to use the information gathered from a patient history and a physical exam.

Texts to Promote Learning

In addition to supporting the work of knowledgeable practitioners, texts play some role in creating knowledgeable practitioners. The designs of texts reflect the accumulated wisdom and insights of the designers. They also shape the ways that readers interpret and use information, in effect training them to participate in a particular discursive activity. The training can be explicit, in the form of training cards and training classes, or more indirect, arising from an individual's use of a text.

Readers respond to the genred information contained in familiar texts. The information attunes readers to valued uses while simultaneously invoking various organizational and communicative actions associated with that information (Yates and Orlikowski, 1994, p. 542). That is, genres are connected to ways professionals carry out their work and interact with others. They carry information about social actions, networks, intentions, and expectations. When readers encounter familiar genres, they are able to form expectations of the text from which they can often determine how to make sense of the information. At the same time, writers who use genres learn to shape information to fit patterns of reporting suggested by the genre. For this reason, we can argue that genres play a clear role in training, for reasons that have much to do with affordances of text that we have been discussing (see also Bazerman, 2000).

A second way genres assist in training is that they reflect the routines and traditions of an organization. Similar arguments have been made about the ways that genres are associated with identity and professional affiliation (Berkenkotter and Huckin, 1994; Geisler, 1994; Prior, 1998) as well as with the structure of organizational knowledge (Smart, 1999). As writers become familiar with genres, they become more aware of the organizational identity, expectations regarding their relationships to colleagues, and the ways that the organization "thinks" and reacts to recurring rhetorical situations. Professionals who use genres to guide their writing practices interact, in effect, with others in the organization whose interests are also tied to those genres.

Texts to Support Adaptation

The qualities that make texts useful for preserving and disseminating information create problems as well. Work activity in many organizations gives the outward impression of a single, unified process aimed at a common set of goals. On the ground, work activities are better described as messy, ad hoc processes that compete against one another and make different uses of shared information. There is a need for information to be fixed, to lend some degree of coherence and stability to work practices, yet the information must also be fluid to support more contingent and situated work practices.

Fixed information benefits an organization, but it is important to ensure flexibility as well. For a text to serve the needs of individuals, through whose work organizational activity is actuated, texts must serve two purposes. They must fix information in a context of use, but leave it fluid enough to be used in a variety of applications. While fixed information has its benefits, the more specific a text is about how information is to be used, the more likely it is that someone will be unable to use it for tasks not anticipated by the writer. Henderson (1991, 1998) discusses this phenomenon, noting that the more closely information is tied to a particular use and to secondary knowledge needed for interpretation (e.g., knowledge of specialized software), the more likely it is that some information sharing relationships will deteriorate. Coordinated work relationships will be replaced by dependent relationships, thus altering the nature of the work that is done.

Fluid information lacks a rigid structure. It can be "poured in" to any number of containers that structure the information for different uses. While no information is completely fluid or completely adaptable, fluidity is, to some degree, an inherent quality of text. While some information about meaning, content, and context can be communicated textually, there is always some dimension of meaning that is lost. The reason is that texts flatten information. They simplify ideas, experiences, and insights and record them as abstract representations (Latour, 1986, p. 21). In other words, texts ably record the locutionary act (what is said) but do not over-determine an illocutionary act (interpretation of what is meant) (Olson, 1996, p. 93). Texts can be used at a number of cross-purposes to the extent that such interpretive flexibility is present in the design.

So much of what is valuable about information is to be found less in what is said and more in how it is "taken up" into a given work practice (see Bazerman, 2000b; Star and Greisemer, 1989). Because writing leaves off much of the illocutionary force of its content, its utility is tied to interpretation, participation from a reader in the illocutionary act (Bakhtin, 1986). It is through the act of interpretation that readers recognize the mediating value of a text, and because texts can be modified, they can be inflected with cues to assist in their illocutionary uptake.

Flattened information also provides a degree of flexibility for coordinating cooperative work. Information that is not designed for use by one particular group of readers can supply different information to other users, who will apply different mediating frames to the information (e.g., notes, annotations, software interfaces). Texts that preserve a degree of information fluidity raise the level of their "ecological flexibility" (Luff, Heath, and Greatbatch, 1992, p. 164), meaning that they can be used in a variety of settings and can support a variety of cooperative work relationships.

Texts to Promote Organization

As this discussion is starting to reveal, texts mediate both individual and group work practices. Texts provide structure to cooperative work groups, often by supporting the effectiveness and efficiency of individual work. To explain text's capacity for promoting organization, one needs to look at the ease with which texts support and define work processes and work practices. The former refers to the collective flow of work activities defined in terms of movement toward company goals and the latter to "the activity involved in getting the work done" (Brown and Duguid, 2000, p. 97). Processes are made up of practices, which are the local, improvisational activities that collectively constitute organizational work. As a quality describing coherent and coordinated work practices, organization is achieved both by specifying process and by supporting practice.

Brown and Duguid note that the danger of focusing too directly on supporting work practice is that if those practices are allowed "to evolve too independently [they would] become too loosely 'coupled' to the organization" (2000, p. 115). Attention to the process view is important, for it gives shape and direction to organizational practices (2000, p. 114). Texts are particularly good at both articulating and spreading a process view, while also providing subtle mediating guidance at the level of practice.

Another quality connected to a text's ability to spread process knowledge is its mobility (Latour, 1986, p. 20). When observations, explanations, calculations, and drawings are set in text, that information becomes more portable because it is no longer tied to a context, nor is it locked in someone's head. While knowledge, experience and points of view are difficult to pass on, the texts on which we record representations of that information are easily created and distributed. This mobility has only increased with technological assistance.

The mobility of text ensures that information is available throughout an organization, but capacity for distribution does not account for the organizational effects on small-scale cooperative activities. How does process influence practice? One explanation is that texts help produce permanent cognitive changes in individuals. Another is that texts influence socio-cognitive behavior. These approaches are related.

Theories that posit individual cognitive changes appear to support an argument that, to some extent, organization is a self-forming state and that consistent, predictable changes in the cognitive states of individuals can account for the formation of this coherence and structure. Goody (1987), Goody and Watt (1968), and Vygotsky (1978) advance similar arguments that texts initially structure work activity by providing external support. Texts extend a person's existing capacity for doing a task by providing structure and clarity that is not inherent in the task. For example, decision diagrams extend a reader's decision-making ability by arranging information into visual relationships that make good decisions easier to recognize. Ultimately, the support offered by text and other mediating structure is internalized (Vygotsky, 1978, pp. 90-91) where the structure becomes a habit of mind.

From this argument, it follows that organization occurs in individuals who have all internalized the same ways of thinking about and structuring their work. If the texts supplying this initial structure are faithfully reproduced and widely distributed, one could argue that the texts encourage consistent individual development. The support for this interpretation of the cognitive impact of text is, however, in question (see Scribner and Cole, 1981, p. 229).

Scribner and Cole's study suggests that it would be a mistake to attribute cognitive changes to texts alone. Rather, we should direct our attention to the social groups and activities that form around texts in order to see what sort of cognitive benefits individuals accrue. Scribner and Cole's findings point us to the conclusion that the social organization that texts promote, more than the texts themselves, may be a significant factor in determining how some work practices change.

Scribner and Cole's findings do not utterly dispute the underlying claim that texts affect practice. Rather, they point out that the effect is more complicated than previously argued. Texts do not "produce" a lasting, individual cognitive effect. Instead, they alter the relationships between people and the information they share. Texts create new opportunities for social arrangements and for reinforce existing ones. A similar effect is to be expected in organizations as well.

One additional step will connect texts to practice. Texts rely on reader participation. Readers make meaning by listening to and responding to a text, by adding illocutionary force to the existing content. However, a reader's ability to make meaning is not completely unfettered. Writers shape the illocutionary act by including information that provides some instruction for interpretation (e.g., visual design, use of genre). The implication is that texts do more than deliver information. Texts create, reinforce, and alter relationships between writers and readers. Goody and Watt (1968) and Olson (1996) both note that interpreting texts requires an appropriate literacy. Readers must be able to interpret pictographic or logographic information used to represent ideas, and if the information is unfamiliar, readers become dependent on the writers for access.

In other words, texts promote and constrain readers' ability to "activate" a text (Smith, 1984, p. 70) to employ appropriate interpretive strategies to get information from a text and to act on it. At times, the appropriate interpretive strategy will be to build or rely on a social structure in which the text is a meaningful artifact. Interpretation can be a distributed activity whereby readers bring to bear other texts, resources, and people on the activation of a given text. Smith also argues that interpretive strategies are not individual; they are social in origin. The strategies come from learned ways of exploring texts, from expectations based on previous experiences, and from conventional strategies of expression and usage employed by the writer. In this sense, texts communicate information about interpretation, and in doing so, reinforce ways of reading and using the information.

Writers can plan for their texts to be "activated" in particular ways, expecting that readers who encounter that information will know what to expect from the text, and will recognize how to use it in the organization of local cooperative practices. Multiply this effect by 100 . . . by 500, and it becomes evident that the numerous texts circulating in an organization play a significant role in structuring work practices and organizational processes.

Texts to Help Create Cognitive Architecture

The preceding analysis of how single texts mediate practice, process, and organizational structure indicates the complex tasks that writers face, but the analysis of work relationships between writer and reader disguises the full complexity. The people who write and receive texts also work with other texts, and the texts that they write are in conversation with other texts, creating entire interrelated systems of text that provide a more comprehensive, complex mediation. An analysis of this phenomenon will demonstrate more of the socio-cognitive complexity that writers must learn to address when producing text. It also raises the stakes for writing review one last notch.

When knowledge, experience, and points of view are captured in two-dimensional, inscripted forms, they can easily be "reshuffled and recombined" (Latour, 1986, p. 21). Entirely different kinds of knowledge can be created by putting parts of texts into conversation with others. Soon, these aggregations of texts form networks of mediating resources that extend the cognitive abilities of the people within and across different work settings. The texts and the organizational relationships that they encourage constitute a network on to which people offload cognitive effort for interpretation, calculation, information sharing, transformation, and all manner of cognitive and information processing tasks. This network is a "cognitive architecture" of texts, data, and people arranged to offer the greatest advantage for cognitive and social tasks (Hollan, Hutchins, and Kirsh,

2000; Hutchins, 1995, p. 357). In genre theory, these networks are variously referred to as genre ecologies (Spinuzzi, 2003; Spinuzzi and Zachary, 2000) and genre systems (Bazerman, 2003b). In this architecture, texts become inseparable from the social and cognitive work that they support. They form part of a cognitive network that is distributed across people and objects, and which extends forward and backward in time.

Architecture is a metaphorical device for explaining how texts, technologies, and people hold information and distribute it in time and space. Theories of cognitive architecture (Hollan et al., 2000) begin with the assertion that texts serve instrumental purposes. Take, for example, notecards on which some doctors write patient notes. The notecard text is a flexible arrangement of patient information that doctors create to mediate the task of diagnosing and treating a condition. However, the notecard is not the only text doctors bring to bear on this task. They also consult the patient's record, radiographs, formularies, colleagues, and other medical documents. Each text and person is a point on that cognitive architecture to which cognitive tasks can be offloaded. These tasks might include information processing (converting symptoms to causes), testing a hypothesis, or simply holding information for later use. This architecture supports local organization of labor effort (Luff et al., p. 168) by ensuring the availability of information and the ability to process it for use in a variety of tasks. More generally, cognitive architectures afford:

- distribution of cognitive processes across the members of a social group,
- coordination of internal and external (material and environmental) structure to support cognitive processes, [and]
- distribution of cognitive processes through time in such a way that the products of earlier events can transform the nature of later events (Hollan et al., 2000, p. 176).

Texts that form part of an organization's cognitive architecture make information accessible, allow transformation of information across contexts of use, and generally create patterns of cooperative interaction. The resulting social organization is itself a stable cognitive architecture to which people can offload cognitive effort (p. 177). Information technology adds another layer to this cognitive architecture, which will be the focus of Chapter 3.

Within the larger organizational cognitive architecture there are numerous smaller architectures that structure work practices at the local level. Texts distributed throughout an organization often sit on the borders between different task settings (Star and Greisemer, 1989). They are taken up into these different work activities, where they play central or peripheral roles in a given task. Each text becomes part of numerous smaller cognitive architectures of people, texts, and technologies.

These architectures are not even bound by a single organization. Texts may sit on the boundaries between work settings that extend across organizations, as in the case of clean air regulations that are used between divisions of an environmental engineering firm, state government agencies, testing contractors, and the businesses bound by those regulations. Within each group there are constellations of other texts, technologies and people that combine to form cognitive architectures that inform the work in those locales. Individuals may have their own cognitive architectures, comprised of technologies and texts within a genre set (Bazerman, 2003b) that one commonly works with. The architectures may be as small as the limited ecology of resources available at a writer's desk.

The point of concern with regard to writing review is the social interaction that is supported and constrained by these architectures. Bazerman describes the cumulative interaction within and between cognitive architecture as a genre system that is "comprised of the several genre sets of people working together in an organized way, plus the patterned relations in the production, flow, and use of these documents" (2003b, p. 318). The multiplicity of texts and genres guides how individuals interact with the objects of their work and how they interact with each other.

Collectively, these texts form a significant part of a person's awareness of how work gets done. In this way, texts play a significant and complex role in formatively shaping both work practices and processes. Texts contribute to the formation of "discourse," referring to "forms of communication and interrelation that are mediated by documents" (Smith, 1984, p. 63) that "[create] forms of social consciousness that are extra-local and externalized vis-à-vis the local subject" (1984, p. 63). The connection to social consciousness is important, because one's awareness of discourse ought to mediate daily activities, including writing.

Texts provide information. They preserve information. They establish and reinforce ways of understanding and applying information in work practice. They create a perceptual frame through which individuals interpret their own work in coordination with that of others. These points speak directly to the question I posed at the start of this chapter: how does one's writing create organization? The answer is that by writing, professionals actively contribute to a variety of cognitive architectures that mediate access to information. The same architectures also mediate the working relationships between colleagues, clients, vendors, and managers among many others. If an organization is comprised, in part, of these relationships, then writers do actually "write" their organizations, in perhaps hundreds of invisible ways.

The cognitive architectures on which people offload work effort are not self-sustaining. Instead, people maintain those structures and repair coordination breakdowns. When the system no longer offers useful ways to distribute cognitive or physical effort, the architecture will need to be altered. New genres may evolve to make different information available, in a different form, which could produce other information sharing relationships that are more productive. Professional writers and professionals who write play a significant role in building and maintaining these architectures.

It is in this context that we need to discuss the importance of writing and the function of writing review for supporting the instruction of newcomers. It is impossible to think about the production of text as a simple process of recording information and getting the mechanics correct. Texts are linked, in a very essential and formative way, to the very constitution and maintenance of an organization.

CHAPTER 2

Writing Review and Mediation

Writing review can take a variety of forms across different organizations. However, a few details are consistent. Writers, including professionals who write, submit a draft text to be read. Often, the text will be sent up a chain of authority to either a more experienced peer, to a supervisor, or to a subject matter expert (van der Geest and van Gemert, 1997, p. 441). The reviewer (or reviewers) reads the text, marks it with comments and corrections, and sends it back to the writer for additional work. The cycle of comment and revision may happen sequentially, meaning that revision occurs after each set of comments, after which the draft moves on to the next review in sequence. Alternatively, the review may be concurrent, meaning that many reviewers look at a text simultaneously.

Citing Lave and Wenger's (1991) work, Katz (1998) has called writing review an opportunity for "legitimate peripheral practice," suggesting that it is through writing review that writers gain some experience of what it is like to write in an organizational setting. The practice is legitimate because the concerns covered mirror those that writers elsewhere in the organization must address. What makes review peripheral is that the process of carrying out revisions is mediated by the reviewer's assistance. Much of the burden for creating a legitimate peripheral participation falls on the reviewer, who should provide the most appropriate kinds of mediation (see Katz, 1998a, 1998b). Additional responsibility falls to the environment and the material tools and resources available to support review. But do reviewers and the writing review environment actually provide mediating support that leads to "legitimate" participation? Some published work suggests that the more realistic the conditions of review (e.g., tight deadlines, multiple-reader review, simultaneous circulation for review, unspecified agendas for review, lack of consensus) the more frustrating (Henry, 2000; van der Geest and van Gemert, 1997, p. 446) and less efficient (Bernhardt, 2003) reviews will tend to be.

One major function of writing review is to facilitate the enculturation of writers into well-defined communities of practice. Because of the highly specialized and distributed nature of modern business, enculturation is more a matter of determining how one's work and writing contributions fit into a very rich context of rules, people, and resources. The development of organization-specific writing skills is an early and critical step for professionals who are just acquiring an awareness of what constitutes literate participation. Through writing, many professionals will come to recognize how they take on at least two important organizational roles: maintainers of organizational status quo, or makers of it (Lutz, 1989, p. 120; see also Doheny-Farina, 1986).

To encourage development of both roles, writing review must address at least two objectives simultaneously. The first objective is that writing review must be a process of interaction between writers and literate agents who are experienced members of the organizational community. Through interaction that is directed toward writing and revision, newcomers learn about the networks of social and labor activity that are supported by a given text (see Cushman, 1998; Heath, 1983). By learning expectations and the constraints imposed on a given text, writers can arrive at a better understanding of how to maintain organizational status quo through their writing. The second objective is that writing reviews must be safe places in which writers can articulate motivations and, with their reviewers, consider the impact on the organization. That is, in any given writing review there is a point at which the review should focus on a text's ability to maintain status quo and on the text's ability to change it.

Enculturation implies that writers must learn how their texts function within the organization. At the same time, writers must learn how they fit into the organization and contribute to its growth. To support enculturation, reviewers must develop means of talking about texts in terms of the organizational contexts in which they are meaningful and from which they derive. Writers must be able to talk about how their literate activities and intentions fit with or change the organizational status quo. Writing review is a tool for supporting these activities. Writing reviews look at texts within an organizational context; however, they often fail to describe how writing practices derive from and form that knowledge.

As the literature indicates, writing review can be an extraordinarily complex and frustrating process, because the closer the writing review comes to mirroring the complex circumstances in which texts are used, the more insurmountable the task of writing seems to become. Ironically, it is at this point that the quality of many reviews begins to drop off because many reviewers begin to focus more attention on sentence-level details, and ignore larger rhetorical issues (Bernhardt, 2003, p. 452). The writers and reviewers alike require a mediating structure that will allow them to control the complexity of the writing situation and create pedagogical moments where writers can understand the organizational writing situation and find ways to participate in it.

This chapter explores the act of writing review in more detail as a mediated activity. Through a discussion of two different types of reviews, one focuses on the text as an organizational artifact and one focuses on the writer, it will become clear what writers need to learn to become literate participants in their organizational discourse communities.

The most appropriate kind of mediation is that which allows writing review participants to bridge the gap between knowledge of how a text fits in an existing cognitive architecture supporting organizational work and one supporting local, individual work. These two architectures correspond to the dual goals of maintaining and changing status quo, respectively. Often, it is not possible for writers and reviewers to utilize both cognitive architectures equally, either due to lack of experience or access to elements in those architectures. For this reason, writing reviews tend to treat texts as fixed information objects, artifacts that either fit or fail to fit in specific work activities. The result is that many reviews address the text's appropriateness of form at the expense of talking about the literate activities that brought it about. Part of the reason why review focuses on surface details is that the local cognitive architecture (i.e., the tools and resources present during the writing review) encourages review participants to see the text as a fixed information object and to interact with each other as if the purpose of the review was to determine the text's fit in an organizational status quo.

TWO KINDS OF REVIEW

As discussed in the previous chapter, a text is a versatile and complex mediating artifact. Within an organization, a text provides the means for people to interact with one another jointly, though separately on a single project, even if each person draws on different information (Star and Greisemer, 1989; Winsor, 1996, 2001). A text is mobile, a quality that allows it to be passed among users. Texts are also somewhat durable and immutable when cared for properly (Latour, 1986, see also Sellen and Harper, 2002), a quality that facilitates coordination (i.e., the production and maintenance of status quo) among all who use the text. In the context of writing review, it is important to see another mediating function of text—self-mediation. As Geisler (2001) argues, writers use texts to work out ideas, to keep track of thoughts, to hold ideas in place while the text is built. Early drafts, notes, and intentions can be externalized and used to mediate a writing process.

The complex mediating purposes of text can help us better understand a distinction that Susan Kleimann makes between the two goals of writing review. "Within workplace settings, organizations often distinguish between revision, the individual's process, and review, the organization's process" (1993, p. 56). In addition to focusing on a text's organizational fit, reviewers should also focus on an individual's actual writing and revision practices. While some contemporary descriptions of writing review paint the practice as one fixated on the shape of textual products (see Bernhardt, 2003; Katz, 1998; van der Geest and van Gemert, 1997), the reason why may be due more to a lack of ability rather than a lack of motivation.

Review is an activity in which reviewers approach texts from a managerial perspective, a more holistic view of an organization's work and how that work is supported by a given text (Kleimann, 1993). Reviewers ensure the creation of texts that are complementary to the work of the organization. Revision is a concern because individual literate practices must be coordinated with what the organization needs to say (Cohn and Kleimann, 1989) lest the writers continue to produce texts that constrain the work that they ought to afford.

As such, writing review is situated at the crossroads between writing and revising (the practices of writers) and review (the practices of organizations). Further, writing reviews occur at an awkward stage in a text's development, after the writer has drafted enough to consider the text "ready for review" (Bernhardt, 2003, p. 448; Geisler, 2001) but before the text is ready to pass from the writer's control and merge into streams of organizational activity. This stage is important because here the reviewer must both change the text to make it suitable for publication *and* help the writer develop an approach to writing that will produce useable texts in the future. The draft text is an obvious focal point for bringing these two concerns into coordination. The text can stand for a stage in a writer's composing process and for static information that serves a particular organizational function.

To meet these dual purposes, writers and reviewers must draw on multiple cognitive architectures that can 1) situate the text as an organizational artifact with fixed information, structured in such a way that supports multiple work practices and user needs, and 2) situate the text as a representation of a stage in a writing process where writers figure out how to contribute. In this architectural perspective, the text must be seen as fluidly virtual (i.e., not fixed, easily changeable; see Medway, 1996) and open to collaborative change.

There is a third architectural perspective. In this, the text is a material resource that mediates the act of review. The text must be seen as a mediating tool that supports a reviewer/writer relationship that is appropriately supervisory, pedagogical, and/or collaborative. While texts do constitute important parts of the cognitive architectures supporting the at-large work of the organization and the composing processes of writers, these are not architectures on which writers and reviewers can rely equally during a writing review. The participants must bind these perspectives together with the assistance of the resources available during the review. This activity requires a cognitive architecture that will be local to the environments in which writing review takes place, because it is in those places where writers and reviewers meet to negotiate the meaning and future direction of a text.

Katz frequently mentions the need to make appropriate tools available to newcomers, especially models of good documentation that newcomers can use to structure their own texts (1998a, pp. 110, 112). The model texts then become another element of writers' cognitive architectures on which they rely for mediational support when drafting their own texts.

Katz also notes the importance of the supervisor as the experienced writer and mentor who offers encouragement and candid advice about the most appropriate ways to approach a writing project (p. 111). Similar claims have also been made for the importance of interaction with peers and colleagues (Katz, 1998b; Lutz, 1989, p. 124; MacKinnon, 1993). The point of this observation is that writing review, just like writing itself, is an activity that is as effective as the cognitive architecture that supports it. With the right arrangement of the right kinds of resources, it is easier to encourage the kinds of reviews that will help both writers and organizations. To provide a familiar example, consider the writing classroom. Factors such as the availability of class time, the presence of a class of students, the free exchange of texts, the openness of computer terminals, the conventional relationship of teacher and student all create conditions in which it is possible for the teachers and students to engage in a discussion of the writing process, to witness writing practice on computer screens, and to treat drafts as fluid information objects that are undergoing change. Substitute tighter deadlines, take away the computers, tie student papers to concrete work practices, and the opportunities for a traditional teacher/student interrelationship diminish, at least in part because the environment is no longer configured in such a way to support that kind of cognitive work.

For the moment we will consider the first two architectural configurations of text (i.e., as organization artifacts, as reflections of writing processes) that result in review practices that I label "artifact-oriented" and "practice-oriented," respectively. The principal difference between the two kinds of review is that the former focuses on the shape and form of the text as an organizational artifact. The latter focuses on the literate practices that brought the text about.

Artifact-Oriented Review

Artifact-oriented reviews are those used to clarify content and verify the accuracy of the information in a text. The focus of the review is to determine the appropriateness of a text, and correct it, when necessary, by changing the text, but not necessarily changing the writer. Reviewers discuss the ways that the texts are used and/or constrained by other people and texts in the organization. In these reviews, the meaning and value of a text is articulated by reference to the variety of users and purposes that give text its situated value. At the same time, reviewers draw on their enculturated knowledge of the other texts to which the one under review is connected (e.g., they share content; they have a contractual relationship; they are sequenced, and so on). The reviewed texts are treated as parts of an existing cognitive architecture that mediates the varied work practices that occur throughout the organization. In this case, review treats a text as an artifact, which reveals both the text's and the writer's "fit" in an organization (Paradis, Dobrin, and Miller, 1985; see also Berkenkotter and Huckin, 1995; Prior, 1998). To help writers compose texts that meet these expectations, reviewers must help writers see their own writing processes and motivations in terms of the organization's interests.

Practice-Oriented Review

Practice-oriented reviews are designed to teach writers *how* to produce better texts. Reviews focus more on how writers produce their texts and what motivations prompted those practices. Discussion centers on the writers' plans and strategies, and it aims to shape texts through a discussion of those practices. This discussion is stretched over a different cognitive architecture, one comprised of writer intentions, previous drafts, experiences, and notes. This cognitive architecture is one that writers create for themselves, at their desks. It is largely private and frequently lost unless writers make a specific effort to preserve drafts and notes. The goal of practice-oriented review is to discuss the writers' practices as members of a discourse community. Both kinds of review are important for writers who are learning to participate in the text-centric work of an organization, yet it is important that their agendas are merged.

Katz (1998a) describes the kinds of knowledge that newcomers must possess in order to become effective writers. That knowledge base consists of the planning, drafting, and revision of organizational texts. This range of knowledge implies both knowledge of product and process. In addition to attaining information about the purpose, audience, and context for a text (p. 110) writers must also be aware of the most effective ways to express what they know, in ways that would be suitable to organizational and user needs (pp. 112, 113). But perhaps the most important observation that Katz makes is that

> The review process can be seen as an opportunity to help the newcomer understand the organization. That is, specific **reasons for changes** can often be tied to the goals, values, or history of the organization (original emphasis, 1998a, p. 112).

There is a certain amount of coordination needed between artifact- and practice-oriented reviews. Demands on the text as an organizational artifact can and should serve as the basis for articulating "reasons for changes" in a text. A common impediment to these merged-agenda reviews is the cognitive architecture(s) on which participants must draw to articulate concerns about a text's organizational appropriateness or about the underlying writing processes. Knowledge of organizational activity and the ways that reviewed texts support that activity is unavailable to writers who lack their reviewers' enculturated experience. The knowledge of writing process is also unavailable to the reviewers for related reasons. First, their experience of writing is often tacit and largely inarticulate. Further, the discussion of practice may seem outside the scope of the review, especially if the people whose texts are reviewed are not considered writers by trade.

To think about the different points of mediation involved in a review, consider that the three types of cognitive architectures involved: artifactual, practice, and local. As writers gradually learn the rules of literate participation in their organizational discourse communities, they eventually achieve a balanced understanding of organizational constraints and appropriate writing processes. Initially, however, there is a degree of discoordination between a writer's awareness of organizational demand and his/her writing processes (see Figure 1).

The artifactual level is the most diffuse layer of mediation and it includes other organizational texts, past, present and future, that are connected by function or content to the text being reviewed. The artifactual level also includes other people who have a stake in how a text turns out, whose work will be affected by a text, and whose interactions create organizational circumstances that create the need for a particular text. The local level refers to resources that are immediately available to the writer.

The practice level includes the writers and their intentions and motivations, previous drafts, work experiences, notes, and other resources used in drafting the document under review. Initially, the spheres of mediation are not coordinated. Writers may draw on writing practices that worked in other organizations. They may work from model texts from other contexts. As writers become enculturated, the overlap between the artifactual and practice levels are more complete, indicating that a writer's sense of appropriate practice derives from an awareness of the organizational activities supported by a given text (see Figure 2). Ideally, it is through the process of writing review that these spheres of mediation are brought into alignment.

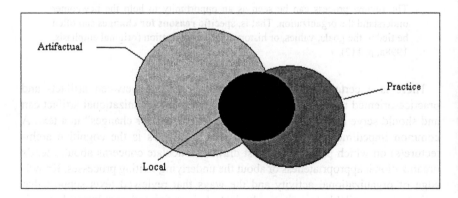

Figure 1. Misalignment of cognitive architectures.

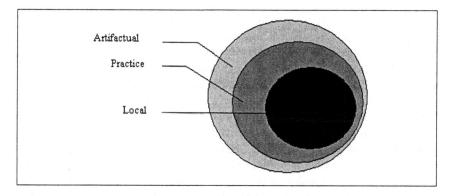

Figure 2. The layers of mediation are concentric.

All of these experiences are grounded in the local cognitive architecture, referring to the local level of mediation that includes the writer, the reviewer, the tools in their immediate environment, printed drafts, and other tools used to facilitate the review (computer displays, pens, etc.). These are the resources over which cognitive effort for bringing organizational and practice-oriented perspectives into coordination is achieved.

We should expect that an outcome of writing review would be to coordinate the artifactual and practice levels of mediation in two ways. The first is to achieve coordination between a writer's textual contributions and the demands created by participation in an organizational system of activity. Colleagues and supervisors have expectations, and existing texts and technologies prescribe outputs of a certain type. The second kind of coordination is interpersonal. Effective writing is not just about finding a fit for a document; it is also about finding a fit for a person. We want writers to see how their writing practices constitute a particular kind of literate contribution. We should expect both kinds of coordination to occur via the assistance of the local cognitive architecture that is available at the point of review.

It is often the case, however, that the tools available to support review are insufficient to create coordination, as evidenced in the following excerpt from a writing review at a university media relations office (see Chapter 4 for a full discussion of the sites of study). The session is a portion of a 15-minute writing review session between a media relations officer and her supervisor. This media relations officer had come from a career at a local newspaper to the university to write press releases and feature stories about faculty and departments. In this session, she is discussing a press release that she had drafted to promote one of a number of "town and gown" initiatives taken by the university with its host city.

The point of the analysis that follows is to show that there is a lack of coordination between artifactual and practice levels of mediation. Note how the media relations officer frequently refers to her intentions and previous drafts as explanation for why the text looks as it does. Note also how the reviewer frequently draws on his knowledge of how the press release is treated as an organizational artifact to justify his suggested revisions. Most importantly, we should note how the conversation shifts between these different levels of mediation though rarely do the participants draw on the same type of mediation to reach consensus about what needs to be revised and how (see Table 1).

As this review illustrates, the participants frequently invoked discussion of a variety of resources in cognitive architectures available to the media relations officer and the supervisor in order to explain the texts and to justify revisions to it. The architecture available to the media relations officer included the notes, previous drafts, and intentions that she used while drafting the text. The architecture available to the supervisor included knowledge of how university press releases are used in local media outlets, knowledge of other organizational genres, and knowledge of concerned parties. There were not enough points of overlap between the two. To accomplish the tasks of explanation, articulation and justification, the media relations officer and her supervisor invoked a discussion of elements in these cognitive architectures, in effect delegating cognitive responsibilities to them. The media relations officer's reference to her intentions was apparently intended to justify why the text was a press release. The supervisor's comment about what editors do with press releases appeared to be a reason why the text should be a photo op.

Delegating explanatory duties to elements of a cognitive architecture is a form of shorthand, a way of simplifying a cognitive task and making the outcome more apparently relevant to the situation. When the supervisor referred to the newspaper editor, he was simplifying an explanation of why the press release would be an inappropriate genre. When the media relations officer referred to her writing process, she did so to offer a simplified explanation of the choices that she made when writing. In an ideal state where the practice and artifactual architectures are shared, references to users and to writing practices would simplify the review discussion. However, because a writing review almost always begins from a position of inequality that can, in its basest terms, be described as an inequality of experience, this coordination gap will be particularly difficult to close.

DELEGATION TO PEOPLE

Early in the review, the media relations officer referred to people in the university community whose interests she represented in her press release. The media relations officer mentioned a group on campus, the RLC,[1] and a staff member from the university's department of campus planning. The people are

---

[1] A pseudonym

Table 1. Writing Review Participants Drawing on Different
Cognitive Architectures

Review text	Practice	Artifactual
Writer: So last Friday they had their preliminary designs and they were talking with people to figure out what they wanted. Next week they are going to present their final projects to the community. Now, they're going to use them for possible funding. So that part isn't really etched in stone; it is just an opportunity that Beth M** was able to think of. And certainly they plan on submitting part of it as plans in the future for funding, and you know to allow this school to become more of a part of this community. There's actually three presentations and the first one is with a very low budget. The second one is with a medium budget, and the third one is with actual [. . .] it was with any kind of budget you could have, although they were still pretty modest. [. . .]		Beth M** is an employee of the university and one of the project sponsors. The writer invokes Beth's position to explain the purpose of the review document.
Reviewer: What's . . . Why do a press release?		
Writer: Well, you know because I think it's interesting that government, the neighborhoods and the school are getting together to try to improve the neighborhoods. I mean.	Writer invokes discussion of her intentions.	
Reviewer: Yeah, but what is the idea of doing a press release that . . . **Writer**: Yeah **Reviewer**: that they'll put this in the newspaper or that they'll come? **Writer**: that they'll come, yeah. **Reviewer**: So you'd really like to get a reporter to **Writer**: Yeah, sure **Reviewer**: to come show up **Writer**: yeah **Reviewer**: Uh		Discussion of how news outlets will take up the story. Discussion used to preface revision suggestions.
Writer: I mean, I don't know if this will work, but my bigger plan is that they'll actually do. I mean I think it gets them a bigger story. If they actually talk to the police officer [out there are they interested, because he has a lot to say. [. . .]	Writer invokes information about personal process, distributing discussion over previous intentions.	

Table 1. (Cont'd.)

Review text	Practice	Artifactual
Writer: I mean, I don't know if this will work, but my bigger plan is that they'll actually do. I mean I think it gets them a bigger story. If they actually talk to the police officer [out] there are they interested, because he has a lot to say. [. . .]	Writer invokes information about personal process, distributing over previous intentions.	
Reviewer: rather than send this out as a press release kind of thing [. . .] The reason I say that is that when an editor gets a press release the idea is that here is something that they want us to put in the paper **Writer**: Yeah, right **Reviewer**: Rather than here's an opportunity for us to go out and cover something **Writer**: all right [. . .]		Continued discussion of the process of handling press releases.
Writer: Well, the reason that I put it in a press release is that there's a lot of information I wanted to get in . . .	Writer continues to discuss her intentions.	
Reviewer: Well there's . . . **Writer**: I wanted to get the police officer and I wanted to get the [Grant Sponsor] grants somewhere in there [. . .] **Reviewer**: Call [local newspaper] . . . Say, here's a nice story about the neighborhood and university coming together and doing something. There's going to be a . . . your reporter can come out and talk to Harold [grant sponsor] . . . Is Harold going to be there? **Writer**: Harold will be there		
Reviewer: But the reason I say that is that it really isn't clear from this that Harold and . . . of course, I don't even know who Beth is, do I? **Writer**: Yeah, right. **Reviewer**: Who this Beth is . . . she could be a secretary. But the fact that she's a resident of [host city]. She's an activist to some degree. She's an architectural preservationist.		Asks writer to consider how well known people on campus are, and how they would like to be known.

Table 1. (Cont'd.)

Review text	Practice	Artifactual
Writer: And I can try to do this as a photo-op as opposed to this and try to **Reviewer**: But even if you did it in a photo-op style: with the date, time, place and so on and what. You could still, under the narrative part, put a lot of this stuff so that they see that this police officer is also fairly articulate. Although I think you probably made him more articulate than he probably is, but **Writer**: Yeah **Reviewer**: But, ***. Now the only other thing that I would change—I would say "[. . .] graduate students are meeting with homeowners, tenants, and neighborhood association representatives." It is much more direct. **Writer**: than "are developing" **Reviewer**: rather than "graduate students are developing lighting infrastructure improvement proposals"—it's sort of like (snores) **Writer**: ha, ha [. . .] **Reviewer**: but I think the real key is what you want this thing to accomplish once it comes off the fax machine. And I think the first thing you want it to accomplish is for people to say "hey, this is something we want to attend"		

colleagues and peers with whom the writer was working, and these interactions formed the basis of her experiences about the text. Later, the supervisor referred to the same person from campus planning, although more broadly, as a representative of the university and as a respected citizen of the university's host city ("she's an activist to some degree. She's an architectural preservationist") who might not be known to the audience. The audience's lack of familiarity with Beth might have contributed to the ineffectiveness of a press release. In this way, the supervisor delegated some responsibility for explaining his revision to Beth.

At the same time, the supervisor made more general reference to positions that people held in the different media outlets to which the media relations officer's press release was an intended contribution. By generic reference to the work that editors do when they receive press releases, the supervisor delegated responsibility for justifying the change from a press release to a photo op. Given the media relations officer's experience with local newspapers, this reference to the editor's job might have formed the basis for solid coordination.

University citizens and their motivations, jobs, and relationships to the media relations officer were invoked explicitly and implicitly to clarify why passages were written and why they should be changed. While the media relations officer may have been thinking about the people as sources of information, the supervisor referred to them either by their roles at the university, in the host city, or by reference to their job duties. The people referenced appeared not to be used for the same kind of information. The media relations officer referred to people as a way of explaining her writing decisions. The supervisor referred to people concerning their expected uses of the reviewed press release.

DELEGATION TO TEXTS

Just as often, although not in the excerpted review in Table 1, writers and reviewers will make reference to other texts in an organization. These may be other texts in a genre system (e.g., air quality testing documents) that collectively create information constraints addressed by the text under review. For example, in one review, an environmental engineer was asked to reconsider the details of his testing methodology because he explained a testing procedure that might have confused the technicians charged with carrying it out. The technicians might then have collected bad data that might have led to inaccurate test results that could have led lab technicians to draw inappropriate conclusions that would not have held up to an audit. By referencing the test reports, the reviewer raised awareness of the related intertextual issues that impacted the development of the study protocol under review.

Many of the texts that writers produce will be used with other texts in a variety of organizational activities. If writers grow aware of this intertextual relationship, they will develop a sense of how their own textual contributions fit within that body of related texts or create opportunities to change the work supported by those texts.

DELEGATION TO INTENTIONS

Another point of mediation that illustrates the contrast between artifactual and practice architectures is reference to previous drafts of which only the writer is aware. In the excerpt in Table 1, the media relations officer referred to intentions that guided her development of early drafts. These intentions were justifications for the press release genre. The cognitive architecture included her awareness of and ability to articulate the intentions that she started with, and her awareness of previous drafts, notes, and conversations that occurred during the drafting period. This information was largely unavailable to the supervisor. The issue that requires our attention here is that the two goals of writing review (review and revision) are distributed over different cognitive architectures, neither of which are sufficiently visible in the text alone.

By distributing discussion and revision collaboration over the artifactual cognitive architecture, the supervisor created a larger organizational picture that was the functional backdrop against which the reviewed text was a meaningful object. In situations like this, the review participants will tend to look at the text as a fixed object that, in its current form, mediates a particular kind of work, works with other texts, and serves the needs of specified users. While such information is valuable, it is more difficult to tie changes in a text's form to changes in the writer's perception of the writing task. Each of these points of mediation is associated with a different cognitive architecture to which writers and reviewers have unequal access. The writers often have an incomplete awareness of the organizational contexts in which their texts will be used. The reviewers are only tacitly aware of their own writing processes. More importantly, because office designs and organizational conventions make writing a highly solitary activity, reviewers have limited or no access to drafts or the rich cognitive architecture of notes, intentions, and conversations that are present as a draft is created.

These levels of architectural mediation need to be brought into coordination with one another. Knowledge of how a text works in an organization is of limited value if writers cannot see how to act on those needs and their own literate interests at the same time. That is, information about the text as a fixed information object in a material and interactive constellation of work practices needs to be coordinated with a perspective of the text as a fluid information object by which the writers carry out their literate intentions.

How can writers maintain status quo and change organizational culture? Part of the problem of coordinating these two types of review goals has to do with the configuration of the space in which review occurs. Bernhardt also notes these problems, summarizing them as problems in the way that writing review is framed and supported as an organizational practice (who reviews, why, when, where, and how). Writers hang on to their drafts; reviews are done by committee; reviewers don't devote sufficient time to review; authors expect few needed revisions (pp. 447-452). The result is that these conditions encourage reviews that are sometimes contradictory and superficial. In these situations, one can hardly expect writers to learn to engage in the legitimate peripheral practices that Katz (1998) suggests are possible and desirable. Problems with coordination can be traced to the structure and context of review itself, implying that review practice can be changed by altering the means by which it is supported. In fact, a number of Bernhardt's (2003) suggestions for improving review practices involve restructuring review by changing when it occurs (p. 455) who reads the documents (p. 461) and what tools reviewers can use to make comments and request changes (p. 465). It is this last aspect of tool use to which the next chapter turns.

Tools that support review practices can favor either sequential or concurrent review, and the mechanisms for comment can either restrict or enhance reviewers' options for suggesting changes. Electronic review tools can either make review a private activity, centered on the author, or open the review process as a public, collaborative activity, centered on the team (p. 465). These reconfigurations of the local cognitive architecture can change the mediated ways in which review is carried out, because they expand and contract the cognitive architecture over which the process of conducting a review is stretched. A desirable change is that the altered conditions of writing review would encourage different relationships between writers and reviewers that would reflect both pedagogical and organizational goals.

THE ROLE OF REVIEWERS

The character of writer/reviewer relationships is colored by the available means of supporting those relationships. For example, when reviewers justify revisions to a text by reference to their enculturated experiences with people and other texts in an organization, the writer/review relationship is potentially more directive and supervisory. If the knowledge needed to justify revisions is available only to one person, there will be a very limited basis for discussion and coordination. Furthermore, considering that writing review is an organizationally sanctioned practice, with a clear power differential (i.e., the reviewer speaks on behalf of the organization), it would appear natural for a reviewer to act in a more supervisory and directive manner. This relationship between the configuration of workspace and the kinds of relationships that develop there is similar in nature to an example from Ed Hutchins' (1995) study of navigation teams on a naval vessel.

Hutchins' example concerns the interrelated job duties of the bearing taker, the plotter, and the bearing time-recorder (1995, pp. 265-266). The work duties of the bearing taker, the plotter, and the bearing time-recorder are all necessary parts of the larger task of navigating a large vessel. The knowledge required for these three positions illustrates how knowledge is distributed in a partially overlapping manner that supports specific working relationships. On the deck of the ship, the bearing taker measures the distance to three landmarks in order to form the three points of a fix triangle. As the bearing takers call out the measurements, they are recorded and assigned times by the bearing time-recorder. The plotter then puts these bearings on a nautical chart to plot the ship's position and course. As Hutchins points out, the bearing time-recorder knows something about the work that bearing takers do because he used to be a bearing taker. The bearing takers, by virtue of their interaction with the bearing time-recorder, know something about the work that bearing time-recorders do. Because the bearing time-recorder shares the same knowledge base as the bearing takers, he can recognize errors in the bearing takers' performance with respect to providing bearings that will be useful to the plotter, about whose job the bearing takers know very little, if anything. The second observation is that the bearing time-recorder and the plotter work together in the same room. The bearing takers are out on the ship's deck. The bearing time-recorder is connected to the bearing takers through a phone line.

The point of this illustration is that because the knowledge needed for navigation overlaps downward (i.e., the plotter knows the job of the bearing time-recorder and the bearing takers, the reverse is not true), and because the bearing takers do not share the same workspace as the plotter and bearing time-recorder, there is a dynamic set up in which the bearing time-recorder can and does interact with the bearing takers in a supervisory manner.

The upward flow of information from the bearing taker to the plotter only allows certain kinds of interpersonal interactions. Because the bearing time-recorder and bearing taker share knowledge of how to take bearings, they can collaborate on that work. However, because the bearing time-recorder also has some knowledge of what the plotter does, he/she can draw on that information (e.g., the landmarks will result in a skewed fix triangle), request changes from the bearing takers and also operationalize those needs (e.g., shoot new bearings). Unlike the example of the writing review, to which I am comparing this illustration, the bearing time-recorder is "present" as the bearing-takers are taking the bearings (if only through a phone line) and so they have limited access to the cognitive architectures on which the bearing-takers rely for performing their jobs.

The case of writing review is very similar, although the degree of overlapping knowledge bases is somewhat different. In many cases, the reviewers used to be (or still are) writers and so know something about the work that the writers do. However, because writing is a largely solitary activity, the reviewer's knowledge of how writers work is incomplete. The reviewers are more explicitly familiar with the work that others in the organization do and so have knowledge about the work that a writer's text should support.

The reviewer looks at a writer's text, recognizes that some information may prevent others from using the text appropriately (e.g., field technicians will not know how to implement a testing procedure) and will communicate that caution to the writers in the form of revision directives. However, because the reviewers have an incomplete awareness of the process by which a text was composed, it is more difficult to operationalize those required changes in terms of actual writing practices. Similarly, writers initially have very little organizational awareness guiding their writing processes. The partial, downward overlap in knowledge sets up the reviewer as a supervisor and gatekeeper, as the person who knows how a text will be used and who is the best qualified to change it, but who is also challenged to share that information.

To use an example alluded to earlier, one environmental engineer was writing a study protocol for measuring air quality at a commercial property. As a newcomer to his division, the engineer had little familiarity with the knowledge and interests of the field technicians and the lab technicians who would receive and process the results of the air quality tests. The reviewer did know about the needs of the field and lab technicians. And as someone who had written study protocols in the past, the reviewer had some awareness of the process by which the engineer had produced his protocol. Not having collaborated with the engineer in drafting the protocol under review, however, the reviewer did not approach the text from the same vantage point (i.e., as an object of writing process).

As a result, the lack of overlap led the reviewer to make outright changes to the protocol that were based on his enculturated experience of how the protocol and its results would be used throughout the organization. These revisions were not consistently accompanied by specific advice for carrying them out.

> **Writer** And you know, now that we are just talking here—there is another way that just occurred to me that we may just want to get some kind of dipper or something that is sterilized—that we know is completely clean, and then fill it up that way.
>
> **Reviewer** Okay, well, I'm going to leave the methodology of how you get the sample and the integrity of the sample up to you. You just need to verify with the lab that the method you use is attemptable and that it is foolproof in case we ever had testing audit. That is what I expect you to do.
>
> **Writer** Yeah, the lab is very good about that.
>
> **Reviewer** So we are talking strategy and I am assuming that the methodology that you use will have been thought out and corroborated by whoever is going to do the actual analysis. So that is a question of chain of custody or handling and that is all done before hand and it should be in here.
>
> **Writer** That's right, that is something I want to do, but I just haven't had time to. I want to put in the exact methodology (Engineering, Simon, Text).

It is clear from the reviewer's remarks that he was aware of how the study protocol and the data that it engenders would be used throughout the organization. The engineer was reminded to "verify with the lab that the method [he plans to] use is attemptable and that is it foolproof." But how will the engineer do that? What effect will the reviewer's admonishment have on the steps that the engineer takes to compose his protocol? Clearly someone in the lab should review the result, but how should the protocol be written in preparation? What lesson should the engineer take to apply toward future study protocols?

The general point to take from this discussion of distributed knowledge is that the work relationships, the ways that people coordinate their work to get things done, are shaped by the ways that knowledge is distributed in that relationship, both in the head and in physical resources. When two people draw upon cognitive architectures and knowledge bases that are not equally available, there will be fewer opportunities for coordination and more opportunities for the reviewers to focus on changes to the text rather than on changes to writing processes. To some extent, these problems with work relationships and coordination can be addressed by altering the means of technological mediation available during review. If, for example, review took place as the writer was starting to draft, the degree of overlap between what the reviewer and writer knew about the writing process would be greater, creating more common ground, thereby creating conditions in which reviewers may be better able to act as peers, in addition to acting as supervisors.

Reviewing a text as an organizational artifact, with fixed form, requires a different kind of writer/reviewer relationship than when the focus is on writing process and on determining how to meet organizational need through specific writing practices.

In situations where the text must be fitted to organizational need, the following reviewer roles are appropriate and common:

- *Supervisors*: assessing how a text represents the interests of the organization. They know how others use the texts and can change them to fit those purposes.
- *Experts*: assessing the correctness and the completeness of the information in a text. They have knowledge of the content and can correct what is missing, incomplete, or inaccurate.

Neither of these roles requires the reviewers to address issues of writing process. For example, in the event that an expert reviews a draft document but has little awareness of the rhetorical issues that the writer considered, the relationship has the potential to be uncoordinated. The expert identifies gaps in the accuracy and completeness of the information and either adds the information or asks the writer to do so. If the discussion never touches on matters of audience, perception, usability or other issues that the writer may have grappled with, the methods by which the text can be supplemented or corrected are potentially at odds with the writer's intentions. The writers, who often lack this subject matter expertise and organizational awareness, must defer to the reviewers, whose understanding of appropriateness extends to the artifact level cognitive architecture in which a text is treated as a fixed organizational artifact (see Figure 3).

In an artifact-oriented review, the distribution of knowledge about writing and about organizational exigencies encourages an interaction between reviewer and writer that is more directive and supervisory, not collaborative and generative as might be expected if a goal of the review is to scaffold a writer's development as a literate participant in text-dependent organizational work. As indicated in Figure 3, the writer lacks the reviewer's awareness of organizational reasons for critiquing the text under review. The writer relies on the reviewer's ability to articulate the important points via the writing review. However, because the reviewer has limited access to the cognitive architecture of writing experience, he/she will have limited ability to articulate organizational exigencies in the form of operationalized writing practices.

The legitimate peripheral practice that Katz (1998) rightly indicates is possible and desirable requires guidance from more experienced practitioners (see

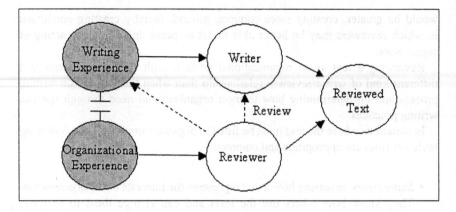

Figure 3. Reviewer applies organizational experience to
a reading of the text.

Vygotsky, 1978, pp. 84-91) that is hands-on and cooperative in its application
(see Howard, 1982). Often, it is not enough to be *told*. Writers must also be *shown*
what to do. A large part of doing something right, writing included, consists of
developing an awareness of what constitutes legitimate participation. To assist
the writers in the revision process, it is important to encourage peer-to-peer,
cooperative interaction, whereby the writers and reviewers treat the text as a fluid
information object, one whose form is not yet decided.

For reviewers and writers to determine the most appropriate way of developing
a text and making a literate contribution, it is more important for reviewers to act
as peers whose concrete advice comes from their similar writing experiences
(van der Geest and van Gemert, 1997, p. 441) (see Figure 4).

As suggested previously, one problematic aspect of review may be institutional, when drafts are shared and with whom. Sharing drafts late in the drafting
process may encourage writers to avoid talking about writing process issues,
ensuring that revisions which challenge a writer's initial rhetorical assumptions
will be seen as particularly frustrating and troublesome. Review conditions
that encourage discussion of rhetorical issues and writing process issues may
encourage better, more consistent writing (Bernhardt, 2003, pp. 458-459) but
as Bernhardt's analysis demonstrates, changing when drafts are submitted for
review is only part of the answer. Also needed is a structure (material/social)
that encourages working relationships between reviewers and writers in which
organizational-level concerns are coordinated with concrete writing practices.

One writer/reviewer relationship that is often advocated, but infrequently supported, is a pedagogical one in which reviewers interact with writers as experienced colleagues and in doing so, walk writers through particularly troublesome
texts. In fact, Katz (1998b) has suggested "the supervisor's role as reviewer or

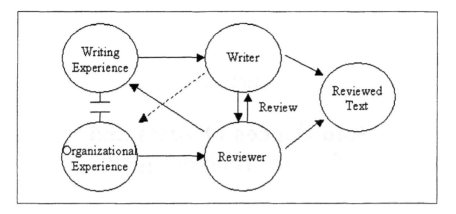

Figure 4. Ideal review allows writers and reviewers access
to different cognitive architectures.

editor may be one of the most significant mechanisms for *teaching* [emphasis added] newcomers how to write appropriately in the organization" (p. 170). However, because of the timing of the review and the manner in which writing has become a privatized activity, the emphasis on review has gravitated toward a concern with "the composed product rather than the composing process; . . . strong concern with usage (syntax, spelling, punctuation) and with style (economy, clarity, emphasis)" (Young, 1978, p. 31). To some degree, organizational practices of review will not change by any substantial measure. The shape of writing review is due in part to spatial and scheduling constraints that are independent of any ideological approach to review. Yet there is no reason why the practice-oriented perspective cannot be supported technologically and made a part of writing review practices as they are currently conducted.

As an act of enculturation, writing review is complex and subject to the influence of multiple factors. People, texts, and other motives are involved, and it is only by situating writing review as an activity that takes place in a particular environment and at a particular time that it becomes possible for writers and reviewers to interact at all. That writing reviews often occur privately between the writer and a single reviewer, and are often mediated by paper texts on which reviewers have written their comments, gives a particular shape to the act of writing review that constrains coordination between artifactual- and practice-level concerns.

CHAPTER 3

Affordances of Texts and Textual Technologies

The argument of Chapter 2 was that the problem of enculturation through writing reviews is related to coordinating artifactual- and practice-level cognitive architectures. A third architectural problem concerns the local cognitive architecture supporting the writing review itself, a problem compounded by technological innovation and adaptation.

Mitchell (1995) observed that the influx of information technology is continually turning experience and knowledge into "bits" of information (p. 81). Architecture, he argues, is increasingly reflecting habits and practices of living with and around information (pp. 92, 167) such that participation in these architecturally redefined places is best defined as a speech act rather than a strictly physical act (p. 9; see also Bazerman, 1994). Offices are good examples of the changes in architecture that Mitchell theorized, as they are comprised of many different interlocking technological architectures that are built to handle and process information. Increasingly, professionals participate in these contexts discursively, through their writing. An office is a configuration of technologies and resources that has evolved to handle information processing tasks. In many ways, one can determine a great deal about what the inhabitants of those spaces value by looking at how they have configured resources to process and use text (Nardi and O'Day, 1999, p. 55).

Workplaces are becoming more diverse. In some cases, many different specialized professionals work under the same roof and on the same products and projects. They work independently of one another. Yet they maintain a degree of coordination by virtue of using a common set of technologies that assist in propagating information across representational states (Hutchins, 1995, pp. 117-119). Tools like spreadsheets, calculators, forms, drawing programs, and so on assist individuals in taking what they know and putting it in a shareable representational

49

form (Winsor, 2001). Thus there are many technologies through which texts pass and are transformed for alternative uses. Furthermore, there is a great need for information to be shareable and available in different forms, to allow different gears in an organization to move independently while still under the control of an overriding set of principles.

Workplaces are also becoming more distributed. Corporations are no longer bound by single continents, nor by single work schedules. At the end of a work day in California, an office may "hand off" duties to an overseas office for the "night shift." This distribution of effort is evident at the local level as well. People no longer work communally at mainframe terminals, and are increasingly working in private spaces: offices, cubicles, desks, cars, and homes. As information technologies become less expensive, more personalized, and more mobile, they will continue to support greater privatization and distribution.

In effect, the technological environments that we have created to handle the "bits" and texts around which work is organized serve the needs of distributed and diverse organizations, but have unintended consequences on practices like "writing review." The architecture that supports the use and circulation of text in a complex organization (i.e., the architecture that writers build and maintain) helps create conditions for writing review that slow or frustrate the enculturation of writers. The technological contexts for composing and using texts frustrate attempts by reviewers and writers to make writing review the rich, pedagogical experience it needs to be.

The difficulties stem, in part, from local configurations of technology and resources that reinforce ways of handling, accessing, and looking at texts that hide both the literate activities on which they are built and the work practices that they coordinate. The burden of framing a reviewed text as both an organizational artifact and as an artifact of a writer's emerging ability to participate in organizational processes falls to unprepared reviewers. The knowledge is there, but the ability to tap it relies on building adequate support.

The dual goals of writing review derive from the complicated mediating work texts perform in an organizational setting. At times, texts support highly individualized, situated, and temporary work practices. In these situations, texts are very flexible in their interpretation and use. Through them, writers play an active role in shaping organizational culture. Through their texts, writers create a discursive architecture through which organizational activities are mediated. Over time, by design and by chance, texts begin to accumulate authority and permanence, becoming standards and rules that govern a wider base of work practices. These organizational processes and motivations change slowly, and writers must create texts that will coincide with those interests. By uncovering the complex role of texts, we can see the kinds of information that writers and reviewers need to share.

For a variety of reasons, both writers and reviewers are challenged to bring a fully informed discussion of texts to the table. Some of the problems extend from the kinds of cognitive architectures in which reviews are conducted (Chapter 2). The ability to articulate and coordinate depends on the availability of means to change how a text "appears" to review participants. This problem points to deficiencies in local cognitive architectures supporting review.

AN ARCHITECTURE MADE OF AND FOR TEXTS

Organizations are complex systems of cognitively distributed work that are partially coordinated by texts describing work processes. A standard operating procedure is an example. The procedure describes how localized work practices combine toward larger objectives (Brown and Duguid, 2000, p. 99). Simultaneously, texts enable innovation and ad hoc work practices that are not anticipated by the work process (p. 100). Organizations have an interest in managing work practices, so texts need to be fixed in their interpretation and use (see Yates, 1993). Yet to accommodate the variability of situated practice, the texts must also be fluid and open to innovative uses. Texts are valuable because they can be both fixed and fluid in use, but their dual use imbues them with a degree of uncertainty. The fluid and fixed states change over time and by situation. Figure 1 illustrates these overlapping dimensions of fluidity and fixity.

This graphic represents scope and duration. Scope ranges from "organization" (describing texts that have an effect on the organization as a whole) to "individual" (describing texts that affect the work of individuals). Duration measures ranges from "temporary" (describing texts used for situated and temporary purposes) to "permanent" (describing texts used over much longer periods). The dimensions represent ways that texts are taken up into work activities. On this

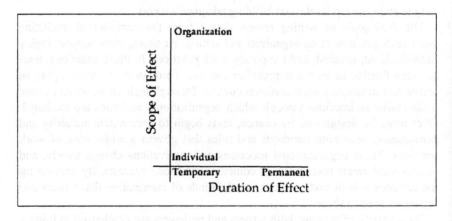

Figure 1. Dimensions of mediation effects for texts in an organization.

graph we can posit text-mediated activities that are, for instance, durable and broad in scope (e.g., writing a standard operating procedure).

The use of texts suggested in Figure 1 is supported by different configurations of resources and information technologies that make the information available as a point of mediation. Texts that support temporary and individual work may be available in highly malleable media and may be instantaneously accessible from a database where that text is stored in both modular as well as structured, genred arrangements. More permanent, organizational texts (i.e., ones that articulate work processes) may be supported by e-mail, file-sharing networks, photocopying, and filing systems that assist in duplication and distribution without any loss of fidelity.

The classification of texts gets more complicated because texts also have trajectories of movement; they do not always remain the same kind of mediating artifact (Figure 2). Texts may initially be used for temporary and individual purposes, but may persist longer than expected and provide constant, more durable mediation. Texts also have angles of ascent and descent that illustrate how they pass out of one person's hands and become organizational artifacts (Figure 2).

The text whose trajectory is illustrated above is a set of instructions that an environmental engineer would provide to field agents for collecting air quality samples. Initially, the instructions start off as a text that guides one particular collection cycle. Over time, this text may be taken up into wider circulation as a description of a standard procedure. Then, as a text describing a work process, it can be duplicated, archived, stored, and shared, exhibiting a downward mediating effect on the work of future field agents (Figure 3).

Depending on a text's significance, it may accumulate other mediating artifacts (e.g., texts that spin off or that report on related activities). In this

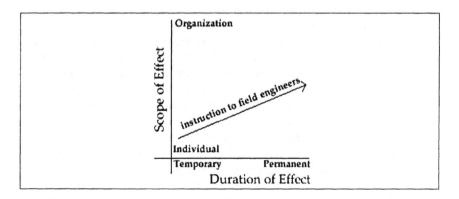

Figure 2. Depiction of the directionality of textual mediation
in an organization.

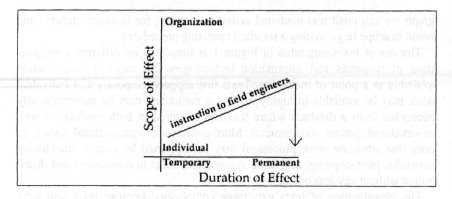

Figure 3. As texts become instantiated in more organizational practices, they begin to exhibit a downward mediating effect on other work practices.

sense, a text can become a node in the cognitive architecture of many different work activities.

Writers are challenged to create texts that serve immediate and future mediating purposes by understanding the mechanisms (social and technological) that influence how and why texts are taken up into streams of activity. These factors will have a bearing on how a writer is to understand the plasticity or rigidity of a text in the near and far future (Figure 4).

In the fluid region, texts are more flexible in their uses and technological representations. In the fixed region, texts serve a process function, by imposing downward structure on an activity. Knowledge of how texts move between these states entails understanding not only what work activities flow through that text, but also understanding the people, technologies, and other resources that form those local and global architectures.

This process of moving from temporary to more permanent mediation also describes a process by which a text moves from being a draft on the writer's desk to a text that is released into the public sphere, where it serves a broader mediating purpose (see Geisler, 2001). In the early stages of development, the text is a draft; sections are moved around and rewritten. The text serves a very localized and individualized set of tasks. It mediates the writer's own progress through the draft. Once the writer determines that the text is ready for review, it begins an upward trajectory, becoming more fixed in form (i.e., it represents a "finished" draft) and it moves into the hands of a reviewer. Upon reviewer approval, the text may continue its upward ascent. That is, writing review is mediated by the same social and technological architectures that move texts throughout an organization. In writing review, however, the tensions between fluidity: fixity, impermanence: permanence, and individual: organizational, need to be simultaneously raised to a

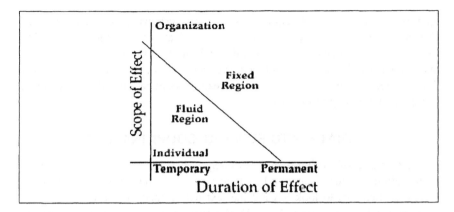

Figure 4. As texts are taken up, their form becomes more fixed.
Their composition becomes more circumscribed and
less open to interpretation.

common level of awareness. Naturally, writing review is difficult to carry out, because the social and technological contexts in which texts are meaningful are distinctly different and separate from one another, each reinforcing their own values.

Writing review will come naturally to some reviewers and less so to others. Those trained as writers and who review work by those who consider themselves writers may easily discuss issues of process and organizational use. Reviewers who lack that training and who review the work of professionals who *do not* see themselves as writers, those for whom texts are merely byproducts of their "real" work, may find review considerably more difficult. Yet both perspectives are necessary for writing review to serve as a tool of enculturation.

Writing review requires, then, a unique technological and social mediation that allows writers and reviewers to examine a text from different vantage points of time, activity, and context so as to engage in the joint construction of that text, in fulfillment of review's pedagogical purpose. Appropriate mediation should:

- Separate views of the text as an individual and organizational artifact.
- Support description of a text's mediating trajectories.
- Support coordinated understanding of a writer's intent and a text's organizational function.
- Create a medium for joint action as a foundation for experiential learning (see Bateson, 1972; Lave and Wenger, 1991).

If we are to foster good writing review practices, we must ask strategic questions about the kind of alternative technological mediation that would be appropriate. This process requires us to ask questions about "core values," (Nardi and O'Day, 1999, p. 67), to uncover motivations and objectives (p. 72), to consider the obstacles that prevent the realization of those objectives (p. 73), and to consider alternative ways to achieve them (p. 73). As indicated in Chapter 2, two objectives for writing review are creating coordination and understanding writing as a literate performance.

MEDIATION TO SUPPORT COORDINATION

The first goal of writing review is to help writers become contributors to the organizational cultures supported by their writing. Achieving this goal requires review participants to look beyond the text before them to see the streams of activity in which the text will sit. Furthermore, it requires the participants to think about the text as a multi-faceted object, one that creates conditions by which people interact and that creates constraints on how related texts develop. These texts will appear functionally different with regard to how they are represented and circulated (e.g., will a text be archived on an Intranet and used at a later date when the circumstances of the text's current context are no longer applicable or important?).

To some extent, the kind of coordination that texts should support is designed into the technologies used to create them. Genres are designed to represent information for specific uses. Templates specify how people can and should interact with a text. File storage systems help determine who has access to information and how the information is to be distributed. Content management systems help classify texts by content and use.

Although support for coordination is designed into technologies, the work is replaced by the tool's interface and removed from sight. Writers do not actually create coordination, they just become skilled at using the technology's interface (see Latour, 1995, p. 263). Consequently, writers may tacitly learn coordination through rote use of these technologies, but the danger of leaving coordination to tools is that it is more difficult to look at and to scrutinize. This condition may explain why technologies, like genres, will often persist in an organization long after they cease to serve a valuable purpose.

Despite these built-in controls, it is still easy to "get it wrong," for writers to misunderstand the importance of the genres that they use, to overlook the importance of templates and controlled vocabularies, and to fail to see how their texts will be technologically represented. Experienced writers and reviewers have a lived experience with these technologies; they understand how to interact with them (see Latour, 1995, pp. 266-267). However, this experiential knowledge is difficult (if not impossible) to discuss directly. It is as much in the hands as in the mind.

In practice, some of this experiential knowledge is spoken through the comments that reviewers put on a draft. Yet in many cases, the marks are only impressions of experiential awareness. The marks themselves are technologies that replace the work of explanation. The marks just indicate that a change should be made.

Writers will lack this enculturated, organizational perspective and will generally fail to see two important details in their writing. First, that as texts are taken up, they begin to accumulate structure or enter into an existing structural arrangement. For example, texts like inspection reports may enter into an existing constellation of textual structure, including permit applications, legal statutes, and previous inspections that point to and create information needs filled by the inspection report. Second, inexperienced writers will fail to see the people whose work is connected through a text. This experiential knowledge can be addressed, but not without help.

Reviewers recognize the features that texts need to have because they are aware of the larger organizational structures into which they assemble. Marking the text with corrections to meet up with these standards is relatively easy, but there is no explanation involved. Only when conditions exist for articulating or enacting those experiences as rules and principles (e.g., a reviewer "explains" a change) will the knowledge of coordination take a more tangible form.

MEDIATION TO SUPPORT DISCUSSION OF WRITING PERFORMANCE

Participation in the text-rich organizational environments that I have described requires writers to develop an expertise that results in their work being recognized as consequential. This process involves recognizing how to coordinate individual goals with organizational needs. First, the writer can come to understand how to contribute. Second, the writer can come to understand how it is possible to create organizational culture by participating differently.

The writing review is ostensibly a mechanism set up to talk about writing process, especially because it occurs at a transition point in a text's development. The text is moving from the private space of the writer's desk to a semi-public space at the review. At this point, the text also begins to take on semi-permanent shape, being delivered as a printed document or one that is at least formatted as it will eventually be circulated (i.e., as opposed to an outline or a series of notes).

In part, the subject of the review is the writer's composing performance. The purpose of a review is to identify changes and, ideally, to strategize or carry out revisions. Writers learn from their reviewers when this process of interrogating the text and making revisions is a joint process where, figuratively speaking, the reviewer is guiding the writer's hands. Yet common configurations of technologies and resources make this joint action difficult to achieve. Writing takes place in private and at some point in the past, before the review occurs. By the time the writer submits for a review, the writing performance is largely finished. Any information that the writer can recall about the process must be reconstructed from memory (a sometimes faulty and selective process). The reviewers are equally disadvantaged, only having the "finished" text from which to look back at process. It is far easier for reviewers to treat the text as the finished artifact that it appears to be and mark the places where its appearance is inconsistent with the ideal.

Behind the writer's understanding of the ideal text and behind the writer's marks on a reviewed text is a tacit and experienced way of looking at the text and the underlying writing process. Each mark on a draft is potentially a comment about a process for carrying out a revision. Each mark is also a comment about performance. But does a mark on the page, a representation of process, convey the same depth of experience that might be accomplished through true joint activity? It does not, but the whole burden of learning appropriate writing practices need not be heaped on writing review entirely.

The means by which newcomers pick up on the practices and habits of mind that enable participation are numerous. Some information is picked up verbally, around the water cooler, by listening to how colleagues talk to one another and by listening to what they say about their texts and their audiences (Spilka, 1990). Newcomers learn by studying prevalent genres (Berkenkotter and Huckin, 1994; Prior, 1998; Winsor, 1996). They also learn by having their hands guided by experienced practitioners (Howard, 1982; Polanyi, 1962; Schön, 1987). The point is that there are explicit and tacit dimensions of learning that require different methods of instruction/guidance and different tools to illustrate and represent the information that one wishes to impart. Knowledge of genres and audiences can be invoked conversationally, but how can reviewers guide performance that happened in the past and which is hidden on personal computers in private workspaces? The literature on tacit knowledge suggests some concrete methods.

Instructors may comment on a performance (Howard, 1982, p. 173), or guide a novice performance by participating in it (Hutchins, 1995, pp. 267-271; Schön, 1987). The challenge is to create the conditions for joint performance, and unless the moment of performance can be brought into public space, it remains a burden on the writer to raise issues of process.

Just as important is that by raising issues of process, newcomers begin to "individuate" and carve out a place for themselves (Katz, 1998b). If writers only follow directives from their reviewers, the opportunities for making a transformative contribution to organizational culture remains limited. The tacit experience of why to write and for whom passes from tacit knowledge in the reviewer's hands and mind to the writer's. Many of the assumptions and conventions about texts and their uses remain submerged in the design of the technologies whose use goes unquestioned. That is, sometimes review needs to be a place for confrontation, for challenges and for risks.

In some ways, review is ideally suited to these purposes because it is a semi-public forum in which the utility of a text is assessed, but at the same time it is a safe place. The text has not yet been released to the public and writers can feel free to make changes that may be controversial. When process is on the table, people will talk about it. Unconventional writing practices, unique ways of approaching the subject matter, and unique ways of expressing content in an otherwise conventional genre format are just jarring enough to the reviewer's enculturated perspective that he/she needs to account for "the way things should be." Through these little disruptions changes take place, but unless process can be resurrected and brought out of private technological spaces, it will remain below the surface of the review discussion.

For writing review to serve these purposes, the activity of writing must come to the surface and become a subject of conversation. The writing review must also become an opportunity for performance in a way that is currently not supported.

TOOLS IN WRITING REVIEW: PAPER

A successful writing review will need to uncover the complexities of text in detail and create a surface on which reviewer and writer can engage in a joint construction of the text. Just as importantly, a representation of text that brings these organizational and practice-oriented perspectives to the surface must be "simultaneously and equally accessible" (Clark, 1996, p. 47) to all who would use it. This requirement returns us to a consideration of what constitutes appropriate technological mediation.

Paper texts, which are commonly used to mediate writing reviews, fail Clark's requirement for a tool that supports joint activity because they do not "mean" any one thing. In that sense, they are not equally accessible. Texts are constructed to be abstract and applicable across contexts. This is both why they are so plentiful and why the issue of writing review is so important. Instead of having "a meaning," texts instead have what Charles Wood (1992a) calls "semantic potential"—the potential for meaning. But if the meaning that writers and reviewers attribute to a text comes out of either a tacit or private perspective, then there is little opportunity to form common ground and engage in joint action. This is precisely the problem with paper text as a mediating tool for review. *A text does not specifically suggest any one interpretation to guide a cooperative revision.*

Highly malleable and tailorable, paper is well suited to accepting revision suggestions and for supporting joint marking of the text. However, without some means of providing mediated access to writing performance, the writer's motivations, and elements of the organizational context that ought to shape those motivations, will remain dissociated. Like most processes that fail, however, paper-mediated writing review fails in interesting ways that help us ask strategic questions about the kind of textual mediation that would allow writers and reviewers to achieve the objectives laid out here.

Paper Texts and Coordination

Texts both constitute and support organizational activities. In some cases, an organization's identity is based on the texts it produces. At the same time, these texts collectively comprise a context in which the work of individuals is coordinated and through which one's sense of organizational identity originates. Yet it is often difficult to see how this configuration of people and texts permeates the content of any given text—especially when it is isolated from that context, as it is in a writing review.

Part of the problem may be that the context is a mental construction for the experienced reviewer. Unlike the reviewer, the writer is unfamiliar with the text under review. For the reviewer, there is nothing necessarily jarring about seeing the text isolated as it is, and so revisions to its content and form are second nature. The knowledge and expectations that a reviewer brings to bear on a text are embedded in various textual technologies that writers use to mediate composition (e.g., models, boilerplate, and templates). However, learning the formal features of these genres is not enough to understand the social motives that underlie them (Miller, 1984, p. 159; Swales, 1990, p. 137).

When a reviewer assesses a text against an ideal, the paper that mediates the review invites corrections. Revisions come out as direct changes to the text. While writers may eventually learn the social significance of those changes, in the context of a single review they may appear idiosyncratic rather than socially informed. The changes give the impression that enacting them is legitimate participation, but how does a writer learn to apply the lessons more broadly if the review yields insufficient reasons for the corrections?

The politics behind texts and technologies need to become a subject of conversation. Paper texts hide these connections because they are taken out of the activity and technological contexts in which they are meaningful. Furthermore, writing review is only a semi-public activity. The people whose work is affected by the text under review, the other texts that are connected to it, and the technological "public spaces" into which the reviewed text will be taken up, are only marginally "present" during a review. They can be made more present if the review participants are given sufficient reason to talk about them.

Paper Texts and Writing Performance

The more serious problem is that *printed texts (and even static electronic copies) bear little outward evidence of the writing processes and deliberations that shaped them.* Consequently, it is difficult to uncover the intentions, motivations, and rhetorical decision-making that grounded a writer's attempt at literate participation. It is then also difficult to use the writing review as an opportunity for joint participation in a writing process.

Ideally, writing review is a joint activity in which writers and reviewers build a common understanding of the text's function and then cooperate to design or redesign it for those purposes. The result is a writer's deeper understanding of appropriate writing processes. However, composing is a private activity, which limits opportunities for coordination. The alternative is to share the product, a text that no longer reveals the work that has gone into it. The review can then focus on the text as an artifact, but not as easily on it as a writing performance. As a result, the learning process that the review means to invoke is limited to an examination of the textual product. There are fewer opportunities to raise the issue of writing process and so fewer opportunities for writers to individuate.

Connecting the practice of composing to a vision of how the text functions as an organizational artifact requires some cooperative engagement at the level of practice. But when paper texts are the tools used to support writing review, some reviewers will be challenged to get at the underlying writing process, even if that is their aim. The reason is that review and interaction depend on a medium of exchange that surfaces relevant issues and gives them a substantive representational form.

To an extent, writers and reviewers can create these perspectives through language, although it depends on the participants finding the right words to develop a shared understanding. The writers will talk about their texts in terms of writing processes; the reviewers will talk about the organizational work supported by the texts once they move off of the writer's desk. Neither participant will be aware enough of either the writing process or the organizational context to participate in that conversation fully. Consequently, this "virtual" tool that the participants create fails to be equally accessible. The writers cannot fully envision the organizational circumstances that shape the text, and the reviewers cannot fully understand the writing processes, making coordination of those perspectives difficult. It may be easier and more direct to provide a visual representation of practice that can stand as the platform for coordination.

TOOLS IN WRITING REVIEW:
TEXTUAL REPLAY

A tool that provides mediation to allow writers and reviewers to display the text as part of different activity streams (private and public) that make it meaningful would facilitate writing review that achieves its dual focus. This mediating tool would provide multiple views of the text to help writers and reviewers visualize the complex fluid and fixed functions that it serves, both in the writing review and in the organization at large. If this perspective has a visual, in addition to a linguistic, form there would be a solid basis for joint understanding and cooperation. The tool that I propose is a "textual replay," and the mediation it provides responds to the needs that are evident in the literature on writing review and in observations of writing reviews in four types of organizations (discussed in Chapter 4).

A textual replay is closely related to the "instant replay," although instead of recording and replaying a sports event, textual replays capture and replay onscreen writing activity. Textual replay is a term to describe the product of a screen capture program that takes multiple, successive screen shots of onscreen writing activity and splices them together as a digital movie, played back in a way that approximates a writing performance.

A textual replay is a representational technology that attempts to make a text sketchy and incomplete. A textual replay shows the writer's text as a series of steps, decisions, and motivations. By seeing the text as an object in development, the hope is that it will become easier for reviewers to discuss the text's development as a contribution to various task-situations with which the newcomer may be inexperienced.

The software used for creating the textual replay is *Camtasia®* by the TechSmith Corporation. *Camtasia®* resides on a writer's computer, where it is typically minimized in the task bar. When the writer begins composing, he/she "turns on" the video capture by clicking the "record" button and dragging a resizable rectangle around the area of the desktop to be recorded. Any material that moves into that capture field is recorded (i.e., when the writer scrolls, the capture field does as well).

Camtasia® creates the textual replay by taking successive screen shots at a default rate of three per second. The program then sequences the shots in the order that they were taken. When the recorder is turned off, *Camtasia®* splices the screen shots together, making a frame-by-frame video that shows disembodied words appearing and vanishing from the screen. The video can be played back in a standard media player, through which it can be stopped, paused, rewound, and fast-forwarded.

This alternative information technology can be used to enable a different kind of writer-reviewer interaction that moves more easily between practice- and artifact-oriented views, while providing perceptual and representational evidence to which review participants can attach their explanations. It will also create a surface on which writers and reviewers can work jointly, so that the reviewer's experience can guide the writer's practice at the moment of performance as well as after. Just as importantly, use of the textual replay helps create moments of dissonance where inconsistencies between the writer's actions, motivations, and organizational needs can be identified and discussed. That process, captured on tape, has a concrete representational form and can serve as a firm basis for the review participants to formulate an "understanding" and jointly move forward to create a better text as well as a revised way of "seeing" the text.

The textual replay is an idea for mediation that derives from past studies of video (see Matsuhashi, 1979, 1981; Sirc, 1989) and stimulated recall (see Flower and Hayes, 1981; Swarts, Flower, and Hayes, 1984) to articulate writing processes. The trouble with these recall methods is that we cannot assume that the writer's verbalization is an unmediated reflection. Nor can we assume that the verbalized recollection of a writing performance is accessible to the reviewer. Textual replay works within those constraints by seeking to provide a specific kind of mediation rather than trying to remove sources of mediation altogether.

Video has long been used for similar mediating purposes in contexts that range from the emergency room to airports to the London Underground to cross-country sports (Goodwin and Goodwin, 1998; Heath and Luff, 1998; Nardi and O'Day, 1999; Omodei, McLennan, and Whitford, 1998). The appeal of video is that it provides a less selective representation of a performance and a more accurate record than the practitioner may be able to recall (Brun-Cottan and Wall, 1995, p. 67). The video captures activity, and preserves it in an indexible medium that allows people to isolate individual activities or sequences of activities, to name them, and to evaluate them in terms of the task resolution they were intended to bring about. Moreover, Steve Whittaker (1995) suggests that a major benefit of video lies in its ability to create shared perspectives on normally inaccessible work objects (e.g., writing processes). He found that in computer mediated communication, for instance, video may enhance nonverbal communication and the use of visual information to "*initiate communication* [and] depict *shared work objects*" (p. 503, original emphasis).

The video enables what Brun-Cottan and Wall (1995) call "coviewings," which are effective techniques for "bringing the 'field' home" and reviewing materials in such a way that multiple perspectives can be shared over time and across diverse communities" (p. 70). That is, video enables people from different bases of experience to work with the object in the video. And when this video medium can be switched out for a paper copy of a text, the review participants can easily engage in joint revision and writing. Although the performance captured on video is complete, the video allows participants to engage in a discussion of performance that creates fertile ground for over-the-shoulder apprenticeship learning (see Mack and Robinson, 1996).

Further, the coviewing creates the potential for common ground on issue of organizational coordination. When the reviewer is forced to respond to a writer's performance, the reviewer may be better able to name texts, people, and other organizational exigencies that would reinforce or work contrary to the writer's actions and intentions. Here again, there is an opportunity for coordinating individual activity with organizational need.

Illustration of a Textual Replay

To illustrate what a textual replay is and does, and more importantly to show how conversation around the textual replay might lead to coordination between writing performance and overarching organizational conventions, see the triptych in Figure 5. Figure 5 shows successive still screens from a textual replay used to train the writers and reviewers in the study discussed in the remainder of the book.

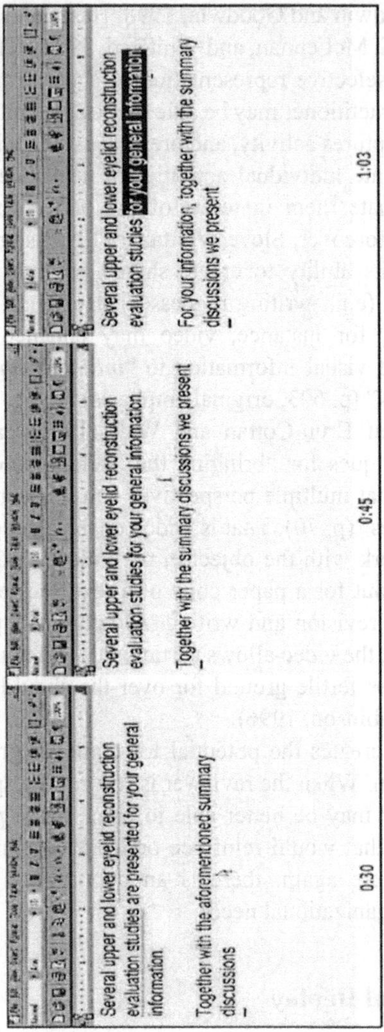

Figure 5. Example of a textual replay.

As a moving picture, these stills, plus the remainder of those in the textual replay, resemble writing activity in near real time.

The training materials differed slightly from the textual replays that the participants would produce. The textual replay above had an audio track that included the writer's conversation with the reviewer. In a review using a textual replay, the writer and the reviewer(s) would supply the conversation. The following is an excerpt from the dialogue that the participants heard linking the screens in the triptych:

> **Writer**: There was a lot of unimportant information, I found. So I was trying to decide how much I wanted to shift there. I wanted to see if I could shorten it up a little bit. "Aforementioned" didn't seem entirely necessary:
> **Reviewer**: I don't think there's ever a good time to use that . . . that word, aforementioned. . . .
> **Writer**: "For your information" is something that I added in, trying to get out "for your general information."

To use the textual replay during review, the writer accounts for his/her writing practices by narrating the activity that appears on screen. The writer can use the opportunity to sketch a picture of how he/she envisioned the text as an organizational artifact and how this ideal shaped the recorded writing activity. The reviewer, who coviews the textual replay, can also participate in an interpretation of those activities by offering reactions, interpretations, and suggestions.

The text shown in the textual replay may become a useful mediating artifact, because it invites a discussion of the text in terms of the practices that led to its creation. It also creates opportunities for reviewers to react to evidence of a writing approach that conflicts with social motives underlying the creation of the text. Reviewers can interpret the activity and the writers can then question, resist, and deviate from the reviewers' interpretations in order to identify issues on which they need to coordinate. In such a situation, learning will not occur in one direction. While the newcomer will certainly begin to see his/her writing practices from a more enculturated perspective, the reviewer will also learn from the newcomer as he/she challenges the enculturated perspective. The goal is that through textual replay mediated review both the newcomer and the reviewer can jointly create an understanding of the text as an object of literate practice and as an organizational artifact.

CHAPTER 4

Study Design and Data Analysis

Up to this point we have been talking about technology in terms of its influence on work practices. The literature suggests that technology changes how texts are produced, distributed, and used. Technology shapes how we look at and use texts. It may be tempting, then, to ask what is the best technology to support writing review? Certainly, there have been many answers to this question over the past few years, but the relationship between good writing review and technology is more complicated.

Despite the appearances, technologies do not *cause* changes in work practices. The goals of our work practices remain the same. New technology only changes the ways that we work toward those goals. These changes vary by settings and cultures and are not inevitabilities. While giving mobile telephones to employees in one organization may lead to improved productivity, it would be wrong to assume that the mobile phone is "designed" to improve productivity. In some cases, technologies that are observed to work in one work setting do not work so well in another setting (Sellen and Harper, 2002, p. 120).

New technologies change the material conditions of interaction in a given setting and alter the way people work toward specified goals (see Latour, 1995). The technologies that we introduce change the "frame" of action (Latour, 1996, para. 10), or the context in which we understand the need and possibilities for interaction with others. Technologies like spreadsheets, mobile phones, databases, and genres change the information's representational form in ways that make some uses of information both easier and more apparent.

In the case of writing review, we can argue that paper texts support a particular kind of writing review. When information appears static, writing reviews will focus on surface details and on issues of presentation that speak to the text's appropriateness as literate participation in an organizational discourse community (see Bernhardt, 2003; Schriver, 1989; van der Geest and van Gemert, 1997). Such a review would favor participation from the reviewer, who brings the

65

enculturated perspective to see "appropriateness" in the design. Such a review would also be less likely to focus on writing process, which is not well represented on the page. Consequently, the goal of the writing review, which would remain "make the text better," would take one route to completion with paper and perhaps a different one with textual replay. Textual replay might lead to a kind of writing review that supports individuation (Katz, 1998b).

Any changes to writing review that might coincide with the use of textual replays cannot, however, be solely attributed to them. The results must also be tied into a discussion of the broader context of use. What kinds of texts are reviewed? Who reviews them? How are the reviews conducted? Do the writers see themselves as writers? Do the reviewers see themselves as writers? In these settings, one might expect slightly different uses of the textual replay, and to see variations in the way that writing reviews are conducted. The first consideration, then, before looking at how to study textual replay and analyze the results, is to consider where the textual replay will be used.

The object of this study was to find out if textual replay plus paper text would mediate writing review in a way that was noticeably different from paper text alone. Furthermore, would there be any difference in the kind of pedagogical interaction between writers and reviewers in organizations focused on practice-oriented reviews compared to organizations focused on artifact-oriented reviews? Does textual replay help create conditions in which newcomers and reviewers can coordinate and engage in a pedagogical interaction that links together issues of organizational need with the writer's literate intentions?

ORGANIZATIONS, REVIEWS, AND RELATIONSHIPS

Writing reviews from five different organizations were included in the study. Potential research participants from each organization were selected on the basis of the following criteria:

- they wrote on a regular basis
- they were newcomers (<1 year in the company or division)
- their writing reviews occurred face-to-face
- their reviewers used paper text to mediate the review process

After compiling a list of potential participants, the researcher spoke to each employee and explained the study. Those employees willing to participate were included. Part of the motivation for choosing these sites was that reviewers and writers would vary in their ability to achieve the dual goal of writing review. The sites split along these lines: those where "practice-oriented" reviews were common practice and those where "artifact-oriented" reviews were common.

Practice-Oriented Organizations

"Practice-oriented" describes an organizational setting where the writers and reviewers see themselves as writers, have training as writers, and see their primary professional responsibilities as "writing." Furthermore, texts produced in these settings are more likely to "belong" to someone or have the author's name attached to them. That is, the texts are more obviously the product of an individual literate act (such as opposed to being an anonymous corporate document). Given these circumstances, my expectation was that the reviewers and writers would be better able to talk about issues of writing process, but perhaps less able to talk about a text's function as an organizational artifact. The practice-oriented organizations were *Metronews* and the media relations offices.

Metronews

The first site was a large newspaper (*Metronews*). Reporters at this site belonged to editorial teams of three to four reporters and an editor. Each day the reporters wrote stories for the next day's edition. By 5:00 p.m., the reporters were on deadline, writing their stories, putting them into the shared network, and receiving edits.

News stories—The stories were relatively consistent in form. Each story covered four basic elements: the lede, the nut graf, the background, and the kicker. One reporter described the parts in this way: "the lede is the news, why we are writing the story [. . .] The nut graf gives story context and puts it in a larger picture" (Stacy, Interview). Next is the background information, which provides contextual information specific to the story. Stories ended with "kickers," which recapped the story.

Edits—A single editor was likely to read and edit all the stories from his/her reporters. On a typical day, it was common for a reporter to write multiple stories. The editor marked comments by highlighting words and attaching notes directly to the story file. Often the notes referred to points needing clarification or reorganization. The editor asked for clarification of content, but just as often asked for information that put a different spin on a story. After marking the stories, the editor discussed the edits with the reporter. The conversation was partly face-to-face and usually initiated by the reporter who sat at the editor's terminal.

The purpose of the edits was to create stories that conveyed information in a short amount of space. The writing reviews were driven by a number of objectives. First, there were artifact-oriented objectives. Stories had to meet length requirements and had to meet other structural and design specifications to be included in the paper. The stories needed to contain quotes and facts. The facts needed to be substantiated. On occasion, points needed additional explanation.

Second, there were practice-oriented concerned. Frequently, the writing reviews focused on issues of process—how to ask the right questions, how to frame a story, how to lead in, and how to arrange quotes. The purpose of discussing process was to produce better writers in addition to better writing. Due to the pressures of writing on deadline, there was a very compelling need for the writers to become effective self-editors.

Media Relations

The second and third organizations were both university media relations offices. The data presented in the chapters to follow are aggregates of data from both offices, used to balance out the number of participants and reviews across research sites. Both offices were located in the same city and both served private universities.

The media relations officers were almost all former journalists. They all had experience writing news stories and were charged with writing a variety of texts for their respective universities. The writers observed in this study all wrote press releases. Media relations officers reported to their respective directors of media relations (both former journalists), from whom they received their writing assignments and edits.

The press release—The most common text composed in the media relations offices was the press release. Universities write press releases to convey information to news outlets, with the goal of getting additional coverage. Press releases are often used to advertise major research innovations, "town and gown" relationships, financial news, or coming events.

With so many demands for attention put to news outlets, the media relations officers had to decide when an event warranted a press release or a different kind of publication (e.g., a photo-op) that would require a smaller commitment from the news outlet. Writers had to consider both the university's interests and those of the news outlets. The media relations officers conveyed the facts of the events in ways that highlighted their newsworthiness. The persuasive appeal of a press release depended on adherence to the 5 W's: Who, What, Where, When, and Why.

The media relations specialists also needed to portray the university and its members in a way that met their interests and fostered a positive ethos.

Reviews—The directors of media relations conducted reviews that left the content of the press releases intact. They often addressed issues of institutional ethos conveyed in the texts, the words selected, and the tone of that content. On the basis of their former experience as journalists, the media relations officers were generally able to cover their subjects well. The reviews focused instead on artifactual concerns, dealing with how the press release would be used at the different news outlets to which it was released. Many media relations officers had limited experience with press releases and limited knowledge of how press releases would be used in different news media (e.g., television, radio, print).

The reviews had practice-oriented concerns as well. While the media relations specialists could handle the five W's effectively, most had limited experience writing for a university.

Artifact-Oriented Organizations

"Artifact-oriented" describes an organizational setting where the writers and reviewers do not see themselves as writers, do not necessarily have training as writers, and do not see their primary vocation as "writing." Texts produced in these settings are likely to be anonymous, group-written, single-sourced, and/or ghostwritten. That is, individual writers are less likely to feel a sense of ownership. In this kind of setting, my expectation is that reviewers and writers would be better able and more inclined to talk about a text's appropriateness as an organizational artifact and less likely to talk about issues of writing process. The artifact-oriented organizations were Donor Relations and the Environmental Engineering Agency.

Donor Relations

The fourth site was a donor relations office in a large, private university. The role of the donor relations office was to solicit and process donations from individuals and corporations. They considered their primary vocation to be donor relations and the processing of contributions. The texts that these donor relations officers wrote reflected a strict division of labor in the office. Some officers dealt with solicitation and confirmation letters; others dealt with texts that proposed uses for the donations. Still others dealt with the legal documents involved with receiving the money.

Solicitation and justification letters—In these texts, the university asked for donations and described the ways that the money would be allocated. Generally, the writers began their letters by acknowledging previous gifts from the donor. In the justification portion of the letter, the writer explained how the money would support an initiative on campus. The justification was a more specific reason for donating. For this reason, the justification was tied to a current academic or research mission, or to a project that was particularly important to the donor.

Contracts and planning texts—The contracts were legal texts that stipulated the terms of large donations and those involving the transfer of stocks and other assets. These texts required the writers to research the company or the individual making the donation in order to ensure that the donation, and the means by which the donation would be made, were conducted legally. The writers then articulated the legal stipulations of the transaction, including a specification of when the funds would arrive, in what increments, and in what form.

The writers also created planning texts that examined how best to reach out to alumni and organize fund-raising events. Although such texts were written less frequently, they still played an important role in the work of the donor relations office.

Reviews—Writing reviews took place within a hierarchy of reviewers. The donor relations office was split into functional divisions (e.g., writers who solicited funds from private industry and those who solicited funds from individuals), but there was one director of communication who supervised the divisions. Within each division, there was a division supervisor who was responsible for reviewing the work produced by writers in that division.

During the review of solicitation and justification texts, the division supervisor read the texts and focused significant energy on artifact-oriented issues. The division supervisor discussed how the intended audience would react to the information, the justification, and the tone. The division supervisor also helped the writers to understand what the audience wanted to hear, and to understand any concerns that audience might have had. Frequently, the solicitation and justification letters were ghostwritten for university officials. For this reason, the writing review focused on details of presentation, to ensure that the letters spoke in a consistent and recognizable voice, compared to previous letters to the same donor.

Practice-oriented concerns were less prevalent, perhaps because the writers and the reviewers did not consider themselves writers. However, it is clear that a significant amount of writing skill was required for the donor relations officers to produce effect letters.

The review of contracts focused on artifactual issues as well, especially because the contracts were legal artifacts that would circulate through the university and coordinate the actions of different departments. The division supervisor ensured that all legal issues had been resolved before the university committed to the donation. She was especially concerned with the wording of any legal obligations. The contract also covered the legal and financial processes by which a donation was to be completed. The accuracy of those processes had to be verified. Practice based issues were infrequently raised, although there were process-related questions related to the development of the contract.

For the review of the planning text, the division supervisor acted as a manager, and tried to ensure that the writer was aware of the interests that other parties brought to the fundraising process. The review was an occasion to talk at the meta-level about the donor relation practices that were common, and which had been in place for years. The review moved from a consideration of the text as a planning text to one that would mediate the work of the donor relations office.

Engineering Agency

The final site was an engineering agency. The engineering agency was a multi-disciplinary engineering office that worked on a variety of engineering projects. The engineering agency was split into multiple divisions.

The division selected for this study wrote texts on air quality testing and code enforcement. Periodically, members of this division were required to inspect industries around the state to determine if they were compliant with air quality standards. If the industry was in compliance, the engineering agency issued a permit to certify the fact.

Study protocol—In a study protocol, an engineer would articulate a methodology for collecting air quality samples. The aim was to assist field agents in collecting samples that would be of sufficient quality and quantity for lab analysis. Secondarily, the protocol helped ensure that lab results could stand up as "evidence" that a company had met or failed to meet air quality standards. These artifactual concerns were of primary importance to the reviewers.

Regulations—Another engineer revised the wording of state air quality regulations. These regulations periodically needed review and amendment in order to stay current with state legislation. When the regulations were amended, the engineer was obligated to go through the text to determine if the amendments were appropriate. In this writing situation, the engineer scrutinized the wording and made sure that it was clear and accurate. However, because these regulations were legal texts, there was also an underlying interest in assessing legal accuracy.

The regulations were anonymous documents; ones that had legal standing and so were not associated with any one engineer. The artifactual concerns largely dealt with the consistency between the air quality regulations, other tools used by the agency for testing and measuring air quality (formulas, measurement tools), and with other regulations. Practice-oriented concerns dealt as much with the clarity (or deliberate obtuseness) of wording as well as with other strategic issues concerning research that the writer should do prior to making changes.

Permit review and schedule of compliance—The third text was a permit review and schedule of compliance, which was written after a site visit and site study had been conducted. During this site visit, the engineer measured the air and soil quality, observed the equipment, and made notes about potential and existing code violations.

The permit review contained two parts. The first described the process by which the industry created its product, where the product went, what was added to it, where the gases were vented, and where the product ended up for storage. Upon describing the site and the process of work, the engineer created a rationale for why the site needed to meet particular regulations. The remainder of the text detailed the changes that were required to bring the site into compliance with established regulations.

The schedule of compliance accompanied the permit review. It specified a schedule for reaching compliance milestones. Along with the permit review, the schedule of compliance required wording that coordinated with information preserved in a variety of other documents circulating through the division. Writers needed to be aware of these other artifactual constraints and write in a way that would accommodate them.

Reviews—Prior to the review, the supervisors reviewed the texts and marked them with notes designating points of discussion. During the review, the engineers explained the purpose of their texts, after which they discussed any problems composing or circulating them. The primary concern during review was artifact-oriented. The supervisors approached the texts with an eye toward the kind of organizational work that they supported and the additional texts to which they connected. Practice-oriented concerns arose infrequently, yet it is clear from the volume of texts that flowed through this division that the ability to write well was an important part of engineering work.

RESEARCH QUESTIONS

The first set of questions asks how textual replay mediation is different from text mediation. The overriding question is if textual replay plus paper text can afford the kind of writing review interaction that would achieve coordination between artifact- and practice-level concerns, provide the writers with a forum in which to discuss their literate intentions, and provide opportunities for "joint action" as a pedagogical supplement to writing review practices.

1. How does writing review mediated by textual replay and paper differ from that mediated by paper alone?
   - Was the textual replay associated with more discussion of writing process?
   - How is textual replay used differently between practice-oriented and artifact-oriented organizations?

More specifically, we would expect to see changes in the way that the writers and reviewers interacted with one another.

2. In what ways does the writer/reviewer relationship change between review sessions mediated by text and those mediated by textual replay?
   - Was there greater effort to coordinate discussions of writing process and organizational need?
   - Did the writers take more opportunities to "individuate"?
   - Was revision more likely to be negotiated and jointly enacted?

Ideally, the textual replay would provide a representation of writing process that would enable the writers and reviewers to talk about it directly and link it to organizational factors. Furthermore, if there was a greater opportunity for the writers to display and talk about their writing practices, there might also be more room for the writers to propose their own revisions and work with the reviewers to carry them out.

One study expectation was that there would be limits to a textual replay's utility. At organizations where writers and reviewers did not see their primary occupation as writing, the participants would have a more difficult time carrying out reviews that focused equally on artifactual and practice-oriented concerns. Reviews in those organizations (Donor Relations and Engineering Agency) would show more significant differences between text-mediated and textual-replay-mediated reviews. The differences would persist in organizations where the writers and reviewers did see writing as their professional work (*Metronews* and Media Relations), but to a lesser extent. The reviewers in those organizational settings would have less need for the mediation textual replay provides.

STUDY SET-UP

The data analyzed for this study comes from observations of two writing reviews for every study participant: one text-mediated and the other textual-replay-mediated. In total, the author observed 26 writing reviews for 13 study participants. While there are not enough observations to make claims of statistical significance, there are enough to reveal patterns of mediation that can be described statistically. Details of the reviews, including dates, lengths, reviewers, and the texts reviewed is included in Appendix A. A summary of the essential information follows in the remainder of this chapter.

The Review Sessions

At each site, study participants were split into two groups: two writer/reviewer pairs worked with text only in the first review. The remaining writer/review pair worked with the textual replay initially. For the second review, the pairs switched forms of mediation.

Text-Mediated Review

The writers and reviewers conducted a writing review in their routine manner. Reviewers at all organizations typically conducted reviews face-to-face with the writers. All reviewers wrote their comments and corrections on a paper copy of the text prior to the review. During the review, the reviewers explained their comments and correction, and left the writer with the marked copy.

Textual-Replay-Mediated Review

To facilitate the creation and use of textual replays, the author installed Camtasia® on the writers' and reviewers' computers. The writers required access to Camtasia® for recording their writing activity. The reviewers required access in order to see and manipulate the textual replays. The writers and reviewers both required training on the software, which the researcher provided. The researcher demonstrated how to capture and save onscreen activity. He then demonstrated how to use the textual replay in a review (see Figure 5).

For a textual-replay-mediated review, the writers were instructed to talk about the activities captured in their textual replays in any way that seemed appropriate. The author suggested that the writers could talk about the words and sentences as they appeared and that they could talk about their reasons for choosing them.

Often the textual replays were quite long. Consequently, the writers were not obligated to show entire textual replay during a review, but instead were asked to show self-selected portions. The writers were encouraged to select sections that:

- showed where they had a question while writing, and/or
- showed text that they felt was written well or could be improved.

After making two (or more) selections from the textual replay, the writers marked the start and finish times for each. With this information, the textual replay selections were more easily accessed during the writing review.

The reviewers and writers initiated textual-replay-mediated reviews by discussing the review comments. Upon coming to a portion of the text for which the writer had selected textual replay to reveal the underlying writing activity, the writer played and narrated the appropriate textual replay selection. The reviewers commented on the textual replays as they deemed necessary.

Data Collection, Coding, and Analysis

The data analyzed in this study comes from transcripts of the review sessions. These discussions serve as the primary data source to measure enculturation practices and the articulation of tacit knowledge (see similar designs in Carley and Kaufer, 1993; Carley and Palmquist, 1992; see similar research practices in Geisler, 1994; Herrington, 1983; Odell, Goswami, and Herrington, 1982; Prior, 1998). The data was prepared following inductive methods of coding and analysis described in Geisler (2004).

Initial analysis of the transcripts revealed that the smallest unit of analysis at which changes in the type of review practice could be observed and isolated was the clausal level. Each clause was separated and grouped with its attendant modifiers. Additionally, clauses were aggregated together to show larger shifts in discussion topics and orientation to joint activities (e.g., explaining a requirement, seeking explanations, or proposing a revision). The aggregate discursive unit is an "interchange," a unit of analysis consisting of adjacency pairs all devoted to a single topic or joint action (Clark, 1996, p. 48).

Participation

Data analysis started from the assumption that the key to an effective review is a free and equitable exchange of ideas. The coarsest measure of participation was the raw numbers of clauses that writers and reviewers contributed to a review. The raw number and percentile contribution indicated the degree to which the writing review was cooperative. Greater participation from the writer would indicate the potential that he/she was using the review for individuation. Greater reviewer participation would indicate the possibility of more coercive enculturation.

Interchange Initiation

Interchange initiations (who spoke first in a new interchange) were recorded as a finer measure of participation. At the start of each interchange, the writer or the reviewer chose a topic and in doing so established, at least temporarily, how the text was meaningful. Those who initiated more interchanges exerted greater control over conversation about the text. The interchange initiations also indicated which review participant was steering the review during different moments in the review and revision of a text.

Review Content

Another analytic assumption was that the kind of conversations present in text-mediated reviews would differ from those in textual-replay-mediated reviews. The conversation was also expected to differ between practice-oriented and artifact-oriented organizations. Text-mediated conversation in the former would focus more readily on writing process. Conversation in the latter would drift toward organizational processes, in which the reviewed text was a discursive cog. In both types of organizations, textual-replay-mediated conversation would balance talk about organizational process and writing process.

Using an inductive approach (Geisler, 2004), the researcher identified and separated four types of conversational content: rhetorical, process, text, and content.

Rhetorical content included conversations about organizational processes, audiences, uses of texts, and work activities to which a text was connected. This conversation also revealed other texts to which the one under review was connected.

Process conversation included talk about an individual's writing practices, motivations, and intentions.

Conversation about *text* included any references to visual and/or verbal means of communicating information, including wording and formatting (i.e., the text as a designed communicative artifact). Such conversation also included discussion of past or present versions of the text.

Content conversation included any discussion of the ideas or content in the text, independent of the means by which they were expressed. Also included was discussion of the "gist" of a text and review practices in which reviewers attempted to establish the meaning of the text by reading it aloud, discussing the content, or referring to background materials. All content codes are defined in Appendix B.

Revisions

Within the review conversations, one could expect to hear calls for revisions. An inductive reading of the transcripts revealed two kinds of revisions. The primary difference concerned how the revisions were justified.

Directive revisions were delivered as imperatives. Reviewers recognized changes needed to bring the review texts into harmony with ideals and demanded these changes of their writers. Directive suggestions did not require input from the writer. They were based exclusively on the reviewer's knowledge of what a text should accomplish.

Facilitative revision suggestions were more tentative by comparison. Often, these suggestions were questions that invited the writers to consider ways to implement the changes or to evaluate changes that the reviewers had proposed. Both revision-suggestion codes are defined in detail in Appendix B.

Coordination

Finally, the data were analyzed for evidence of coordination. Any lack of equitable participation existing across mediated review conditions or across organizations should also show a lack of articulated coordination in the way that the reviewers and writers spoke about and acted upon the review text. To the extent that textual replay altered the participation structure of review, it should also have an effect on the amount of articulated coordination. Coordination was coded by counting:

- *Coordination-Building Devices*—questions and facilitative revision suggestions. The questions and facilitative revision suggestions were opportunities for writers and reviewers to consider a point of view, evaluate it, affirm it, rebut it, and/or offer an alternative.
- *Spoken Coordination*—mutual discussion of text, content, rhetorical, or process issue in the same interchange.

- *Corrections*—The last measure of coordination was a measure of its absence. Every corrected interpretation or comment was taken to be an indication that coordination was at least temporarily absent. At the same time, the correction is a coordination-building device to the extent that it succeeds in repairing the misunderstanding.

The codes for review content and revision type required interpretation of the transcript data. Working with a sample of 13% of the total available data, a second coder verified the integrity of the coding definitions and the accuracy of their application. The precise levels of agreement were:

Revisions: 94% agreement, adjusted using Cohen's Kappa to .63.
Text: 93% agreement, adjusted using Cohen's Kappa to .86.
Rhetorical: 91% agreement, adjusted using Cohen's Kappa to .75.
Content: 89% agreement, adjusted using Cohen's Kappa to .89.
Process   82% agreement, adjusted using Cohen's Kappa to .75.

In the chapters that follow, a number of descriptive statistical measures are used to highlight patterns in the review conversations. First, analysis of variance was used to interpret interval data, including the degree of participation, number of interchange initiations, and degree of coordination. Second, chi-square analysis was used when the data was categorical, as it was for revision suggestions. Finally, narrative analysis of the review transcripts provided a more nuanced interpretation of differences between the review activities. A more thorough consideration of the analytic details, controls, and statistical measures can be found in Swarts (2002).

After reporting the differences between text-mediated and textual replay-mediated review across all organizations in Chapter 5, Chapters 6 and 7 will examine the different uses of textual replay in practice-oriented and artifact-oriented organizations, respectively.

CHAPTER 5

Differences Between Text and Textual Replay Mediation

To be successful, writing review relies on a cognitive architecture that is enriched by information technology. Ideally, the cognitive architecture allows the writing review to mediate the production of organizationally-appropriate texts while also mediating a writer's critical awareness of his/her writing processes. These writing review practices imply two modes of writer/reviewer interaction, one supervisory and one pedagogical. The data reported in this chapter and in the two that follow suggest that *the configuration of mediating artifacts in a writing review plays some role in promoting supervisory or pedagogical interaction.* The mediating artifacts scrutinized in this chapter are text (supports supervision) and textual replay (supports pedagogy).

More specifically, the data reported in this chapter suggest that text strongly supports supervision and that textual replay may promote a more balanced approach between supervision and pedagogical facilitation. Across all four types of organizations (*Metronews*, Media Relations, Donor Relations, and Engineering Agency) five differences between text-mediated and textual replay-mediated writing reviews emerged that speak to each technology's ability to contribute to a cognitive architecture that fosters balanced attention between artifact-oriented and practice-oriented views of a text. Changes in participation structure, interchange initiations, revisions, coordination, and use of coordination-building devices reveal the principal differences. Notably:

1. **Participation Structure**: The frequency of writer and reviewer contributions to the review discussion.
   - *Text-Mediation*: Reviewers contributed more and dominated most of the review conversation.
   - *Textual-Replay-Mediation*: Writers contributed more equitably.

2. **Interchange Initiations**: Indicating who was initiating and changing the topics of discussion.
   - *Text-Mediation*: Reviewers initiated more topics of discussion.
   - *Textual-Replay-Mediation*: Writers initiated more topics of discussion, mostly about writing process issues.
3. **Revisions**: Differences in the types of revision suggests reviewers articulated.
   - *Text-Mediation*: Revision suggestions were overwhelmingly directive.
   - *Textual-Replay-Mediation*: Most revision suggestions were facilitative although not to the same degree that directive revision dominated in text-mediation.
4. **Coordination**: Amount of discussion in which the writers and reviewers talked about the texts in terms of the same characteristics (Text, Process, Rhetorical, Content).
   - *Text-Mediation*: Coordination was inconsistent on all text characteristics.
   - *Textual-Replay-Mediation*: Coordination improved on matters of Text and Process.
5. **Coordination-Building Devices**: Questions, suggestions, and other comments that invited reviewers or writers to coordinate ideas or actions.
   - *Text-Mediation*: Few explicit uses of coordination-building devices. Coordination was assumed.
   - *Textual-Replay-Mediation*: Use of coordination-building devices increases. Conflicts in coordination are uncovered and repaired more readily.

These same differences indicate the extent to which the technologies of writing review afford a balanced approach between enculturation and individuation.

EFFECT ON PARTICIPATION

Textual replay mediation was strongly associated with more writer partici-pation, measured as the number of clauses spoken in a review session. The participation effect was examined with a one-way analysis of variance with repeated measures for participants. The results are given in Table 1.

These results suggest that technological mediation (i.e., text vs. textual replay) significantly interacted with speaker role. In textual-replay-mediated sessions the reviewers contributed, on average, ten fewer clauses (155 clauses per session) than in the text-mediated writing reviews (165 per session). For writers, the differences across conditions were more dramatic and in the opposite direction. Writers averaged participation levels of 92 clauses per review session in the text-mediated sessions to 167 clauses per review session in the textual-replay-mediated sessions.

Another way to interpret this finding is that the textual replay changed the participation structure of the review. Text mediation promoted reviews where

Table 1. Results of an Analysis of Variance for Number of Clauses Spoken per Session

	df	SS	MS	F	P
Technology	1	14058.2	14058.2	2.47	NS
Role	1	12338.5	12338.5	2.18	NS
Technology × Role	1	23908.2	23908.2	4.22	$p < .05$
Participants	23	331494.0	14412.8		
Participants × Conditions	21	119046.5	5668.9		
Total	47	450540.5			

reviewers generated nearly twice as many clauses as writers (1.8 to 1). Textual replay promoted reviews in which reviewers generated slightly less than the writers (.9 to 1). Mathematically, the textual-replay-mediated sessions appeared to have greater balance in contributions.

EFFECT ON INTERCHANGE INITIATION

Textual replay mediation was also associated with more writer-initiated interchanges. A one-way analysis of variance with repeated measures for participants measures the effect of technological mediation and speaker role on interchange initiations (Table 2).

The results suggest that there is a difference between text-mediated and textual-replay-mediated review with respect to the number of writer-initiated interchanges. This change is strongly associated with technology and speaker role.

On average, text-mediated reviews were comprised of more interchanges (105.7), 71% (74.7) of which were initiated by reviewers. Writers initiated only 29% (31). Textual-replay-mediated sessions were built on fewer interchanges (88 on average), but the number of initiations was more balanced. Reviewers initiated 53% (46.9) and the writers initiated 47% (41).

EFFECT ON REVISIONS

Textual replay mediation was strongly associated with facilitative revision more than directive revision. The figures reported in Table 3 demonstrate the disparity between facilitative and directive revision suggestions across technological conditions.

As the figures show, directive revision suggestions (594) outnumber facilitative revision suggestions (169) in the text-mediated review. The mix is reversed in the textual-replay mediated reviewers, where facilitative suggestions (471) outnumbered directive suggestions (334). Using a Chi Square test of the

Table 2. Results of an Analysis of Variance for
Interchange Initiation

	df	SS	MS	F	P
Technology	1	936.33	936.33	0.93	NS
Role	1	7400.33	7400.33	6.80	p < .05
Technology × Role	1	6780.33	6780.33	6.30	p < .05
Participants	23	47541.67	2067.03		
Participants × Conditions	15	16137.67	1075.84		
Total	47	64615.67			

Table 3. Results of a Chi Square Analysis Showing Directive
and Facilitative Suggestions by Technological Condition

	Directive	Facilitative	Total
Text Condition	594	169	763
Textual Replay Condition	334	471	805
Total	928	640	1568

homogeneity of distributional variation (Geisler, 2004, p. 174) the variation in revision types was found to be significant ($df = 1$, $p < .01$). The strength of the difference is illustrated in Figure 1.

In the text-mediated review condition, nearly 80% of the revision suggestions were directive in nature. In the textual-replay-mediated reviews, the trend shifted in favor of facilitative revision, which accounted for nearly 60% of the revision suggestions in those conditions.

EFFECT ON COORDINATION

Textual replay mediation was associated with more coordinated writer/review conversation, measured as adjacent clauses on the same topic areas (e.g., process or rhetoric). In these situations, reviewers and writers agreed, perhaps tacitly, to refer to the reviewed text in the same manner. They may see the text as an embodiment of writing processes (clauses coded as "process"), an organizational artifact around which various work processes or practices are oriented (clauses coded as "rhetorical"), as an artifact that exhibits particular design characteristics (clauses coded as "text"), or as a frame for talking about content and ideas (clauses coded as "content").

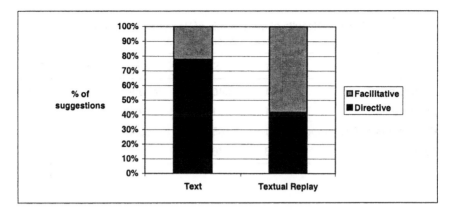

Figure 1. Percentage of facilitative and directive suggestions
by technological condition.

An analysis of variance (results given in Table 4) shows that technological mediation was strongly associated with improved coordination.

The average number of coordinated interchanges varied by mediation type. In the text-mediated reviews, the average number of coordinated interchanges was 19.2. In the textual-replay-mediated reviews, the average number was 38.5, an increase of 100%.

Coordination improved in all content areas, but most notably in text and process. As shown in Figure 2, the number of coordinated references about text increased 158%, from an average of 5.5 coordinated interchanges in the text-mediated sessions to 14.1 in the textual-replay-mediated sessions. The number of coordinated references about process also increased—293%, from an average of 2.3 coordinated interchanges in the text-mediated sessions to 9.1 in the textual-replay-mediated sessions. Changes in the number of coordinated interchanges about the rhetorical issues and about content issues were in the same direction (79% and 18% respectively).

EFFECT ON COORDINATION-BUILDING DEVICES

Textual reply mediation was also associated with the use of more coordination-building devices. Examples include facilitative revision suggestions and questions. See Chapter 4 for additional information. A one-way analysis of variance with repeated measures for participants shows that the number of questions did increase between the text-mediated and textual-replay-mediated review sessions (see Table 5).

Table 4. Results of an Analysis of Variance for Number
of Clauses Spoken per Session

	df	SS	MS	F	P
Technology	1	2403.9	2403.9	15.9	p < .01
Participants	11	5710.4	519.13		
Participants × Technology	11	1655.2	150.47		
Total	23	9769.4			

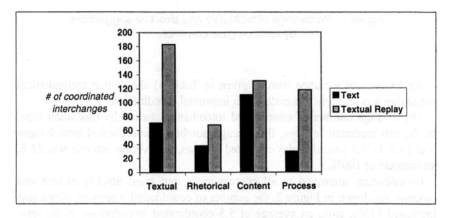

Figure 2. The content of coordinated interchanges per
technological condition.

The textual replay was associated with a 93% increase in the number of reviewer questions, from an average of slightly more than 10 questions per session in the text-mediated reviews to an average of 19.3 questions in the textual-replay-mediated reviews.

Further analysis of the question content shows that reviewers asked more questions about all aspects of the texts under review, but most often about issues concerning the structure and look of the text as a finished artifact (text), an increase of 215% (2.6 questions in text-mediated reviews to 8.2 questions in the textual-replay-mediated reviews). The data also shows a 148% increase in the number of questions about process (2.1 questions in text-mediated review and 5.2 in textual-replay-mediated review). These fluctuations are illustrated in Figure 3.

Table 5. Results for an Analysis of Variance of
Reviewers' Questions per Session

	df	SS	MS	F	P
Technology	1	508.7	508.7	8.0	$p < .01$
Participants	11	1080.2	98.2		
Participants × Conditions	11	701.9	63.8		
Total	23	2290.7			

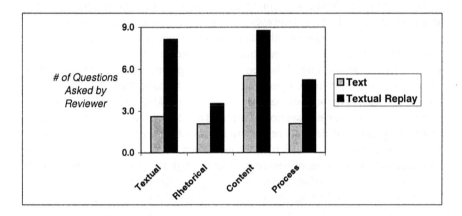

Figure 3. Reviewers asked more questions about texts
in all object domains.

PROFILES: TEXT AND TEXTUAL REPLAY
MEDIATED REVIEW

As noted at the start of this chapter, text-mediated reviews and textual-replay-mediated reviews differed in terms of the balanced between artifact-oriented and practice-oriented reviews. Text-mediated reviews tipped in favor of artifact--oriented reviews that were more supervisory and focused on enculturation. Textual--replay-mediated reviews balanced artifact-oriented concerns with practice-oriented concerns, creating opportunities for writers to individuate (Katz, 1998). A profile of each type of mediated review will highlight the key differences.

Qualities of the Text Mediated Reviews

In text-mediated reviews, reviewers appeared to pay more attention to the text as an organizational artifact. They presented revisions as rules and demands for bringing a text into coordination with a genred ideal. For instance:

> **Reviewer**: I know that we have always said in the first paragraph you should do these specific things. It should "bang" or it should mention a specific reason.
> **Writer**: Uh-hmm.
> **Reviewer**: It should mention other aspects of the gift if there are any.
> **Writer**: Right.
> **Reviewer**: Is it special because it is a reunion year? Or is it special because it is in honor of, or whatever. And whether in the same paragraph or a different paragraph mention if there is any matching money as part of a gift. This is what I call the business of the letter (Donor, Callie, Text).

This kind of exchange was common. To the reviewer, the solicitation letter is a clearly defined genre. However, while conventional practice at the Donor Relations office dictates what solicitation letters *should* do, and what information they *should* include, these conventions are based on the reviewer's tacit and enculturated understanding of the genre. Enforcing genre through the application of revision rules has limited pedagogical value, because the rules obscure the social and discursive motives that they serve. By invoking rules, reviewers allow them to stand in for an explanation of motives and the enactment of those motives in writing practice. Rules may be easy to learn, but if they are disassociated from purpose, one can find it difficult to know when rules can be bent or broken. Consequently, replication of genred content through the uncritical application of rules may create inertia that forestalls natural genre decay and reinvention.

In practice-oriented organizations as well, text mediation was associated with a stronger-than-expected tendency for reviewers to talk about revision rules.

> **Reviewer**: was it on Thursday or Friday?
> **Writer**: Uhm . . . it was . . . I'm pretty sure it was . . . I don't know.
> **Reviewer**: They say that it was on . . .
> **Writer**: Yeah.
> **Reviewer**: Let's get rid of that. The arrest of *[person]* on Thursday afternoon. Right, we don't need that (*Metronews*, Laura, Text).

The reviewer's revisions appear to have been guided by a genred ideal. He saw what information needed to stay and what needed to go. To that point, the review conversation had focused largely on content issues, but when the reviewer came to information about who was arrested, he recognized that it did not belong. Instead of giving an explanation, the reviewer remarked that it was not needed. Not only did this comment leave issues of practice off the table, the revision was presented as a directive.

Qualities of the Textual Replay-Mediated Reviews

The textual replay afforded a different kind of review, one that was more balanced between genred ideals and messier discussions of writing process. In these reviews, the participants treated the text as an object whose final form was under negotiation. The textual-replay-mediated reviews were more often associated with joint discussion of process, rhetorical, and textual issues. This change is significant because it suggests that the participants recognized multiple spheres of activity where the text provided useful mediation: organizational work activities and the private writing activities. For example,

> **Reviewer**: what we want to do with this is not only to simply present the facts of the situation that he is coming here for this, but also how fortunate we are to have this sort of renowned . . .
> **Writer**: Since his ability is unique . . .
> **Reviewer**: Yes—he is internationally . . . so maybe some background work on is this the first in-depth book on this . . . on this person. And if it has won any awards, or if it has been. . . . We will make it . . . we will package it really much more on a 'this guy really knows what he is talking about and he is here at *[college]* (Media, Sabot, Textual Replay).

It is notable here that the reviewer offered specific revision advice, but also connected that advice to a discussion of motives. The reviewer noted that the reason for adding (process) more background information (text) was that the information served the university's interests (rhetorical), in so far as the Media Relations office was charged with serving them.

In addition, the revision suggestion is presented facilitatively, not as a command, but as a suggestion. The writer was not instructed to include more background information; instead, the reviewer suggested "*maybe* some background work on . . . is this the first in-depth book on this person." "Maybe" appears to indicate that the reviewer was open to discussion of possible revisions and not just the one she suggested. At other times, reviewers tied revision suggestions to the writer's practices:

> **Writer**: Well, what I'm trying to do is to research that background to see where this technical information comes from and no one seems to know.
> **Reviewer**: Okay, I understand what you are doing.
> **Writer**: But I should get the technical information to back that up?
> **Reviewer**: It would be nice that if somebody comes up and asks why you were removing that [section] or why you want to make all of the other ones have this [information] you need to be able to show that it makes no difference in there anyway.
> **Writer**: Right (Engineering, Biff, Textual Replay).

Not only was the writer participating to a high degree, he was also discussing his motivations and intentions, thereby exerting some control over the text's semantic potential. The reviewer enriched the writers understanding by connecting organizational needs when he noted that "if somebody comes up and asks why you were removing that [section] or why you want to make all of the other ones have this [information]" the writer could demonstrate that the information was unnecessary. The participants then connected that conversation to the words on the page, prompting the reviewer to conclude that the writer could "show that the information makes no difference" by "doing [and showing] the math." On these types of issues the review participants were increasingly coordinated.

DIFFERENCES IN MEDIATION BETWEEN TEXT AND TEXTUAL REPLAY

The qualities of review illustrated in the review excerpts from the previous section illustrate some of the key differences between text-mediated and textual-replay-mediated reviews. Closer examination shows that, more than text-mediated review, textual–replay-mediated review supports a more balanced approach to writing review, one that supports artifact-oriented and practice-oriented discussion. In part, this change can be attributed to the ways that textual replay differs from text as a mediating artifact. Unlike text, textual replay supports:

- separate views of the text as an artifact of organizational work activities and private writing activities,
- description of a text's mediating trajectories.
- coordinated understanding of a writer's intent and a text's organizational function, and
- creation of a medium for joint action.

We see some evidence that the textual replay meets all of these demands. The remainder of this chapter discusses the evidence:

- Increased writer participation and discussion of process issues indicate separation of writing practices from organizational practices.
- Increased discussion of rhetoric and process as well as process and text is evidence that the participants discussed the text's multiple forms of mediation.
- Coordinated talk about rhetoric, process, and text as well as an increase in questions about the same indicates improved coordination.
- Increase in facilitative revision suggestions indicates that the review became a medium for joint action that supports both enculturation and individuation.

Separation of Text as Organizational Artifact and Artifact of Writing Process

In the text-mediated sessions, the reviewers largely controlled the pace and content of the conversation. They tended to speak about the text as either a good or a poor reflection of a genred ideal. Lacking the same experience, the writers could not as easily contribute to such a discussion and so had more difficulty participating in an evaluation of their text.

> **Reviewer:** My first question is . . . is this for the order or some separate conditions
> **Writer:** Well something is for the order.
> **Reviewer:** Okay, but it is some sort of legal . . .
> **Writer:** It is some sort of administrative order.
> [. . .]
> **Reviewer:** That is okay, but I just wanted to . . . as it is written this leads me to believe that it is for the order because it is a schedule of compliance, but I wasn't sure about the format that you have here if it was going to be part of the permit condition or a separate order (Engineering, David, Text).

The reviewer attempted to raise a question about the text's format and whether it should be different in a way that would allow it to be excerpted into other texts. To make the connection, however, the writer required an understanding of the other texts to which his text would be connected as well as an understanding of which other departments had interests that intersected with his text (e.g., lawyers). Because of his lack of experience, the writer had some difficulty entering the conversation at this level.

The textual replay appears to have enabled more interactive participation from the writers. In part, the difference in participation can be attributed to the way that textual replay re-introduced talk about writing process. To be sure, the study methodology employed here (see Chapter 4) required writers to talk about the textual replay. This circumstance accounts for some increased writer participation, but not all. Although the textual replay required a writer's explanation, it also provided a concrete account of a writing process. The textual replay stimulated writer recall and provided an indexible medium for the writers and reviewers alike to discuss writing processes.

> **Writer:** Well, I think that I viewed this whole template as basically . . . and at the same time trying to communicate change or a justification of that. And when I looked at this "IT Ownership," I kind of felt like, you know, it is really obvious because we are IT and it is our. . . . I guess in previous sections I thought I was already making it clear the type of ownership that we had— in efforts to upgrade, and this is what would be solved, and this is how it would look afterwards. And then I got to this part and I felt like oh, well now I have to repeat.

> **Reviewer**: Well, maybe not. Maybe a thought for you here is to consider whether you want to start out under "IT Ownership" by saying something like "the IT group" or "the desktop support group" has been charged to (Donor, Chet, Textual Replay).

The writer used the textual replay to recall and explain his writing practices and decision-making. He was able to articulate how his actions (filling out sections on the template) conflicted with his motivation to stay concise ("I felt like oh, well now I have to repeat"). Immediately, the writer's discussion became a point through which the reviewer could both offer an interpretation of the writer's process ("[w]ell, maybe not . . .") and also tie in recommended writing practices. Instead of saying what to change, the reviewer suggested *how* the writer might think about and enact changes that were consistent with both his motivations and the organization's needs.

Under other circumstances, information about writing process and earlier drafts would be lost to the writer's memory and to the recycle bin. The textual replay is not an exact reflection of the writing process, but it *is* a different kind of text, with semantic potential that can be jointly claimed by the writer (who describes the writing performance that it represents) and the reviewer (who describes the rhetorical demands that it meets as an organizational artifact). As a more interpretively malleable representation of information, the textual replay allows both review participants to lay claim to its semantic potential and to account for its meaning in terms of compatible activity contexts that are infrequently joined. Review conversations like that excerpted above indicate that the review participants found it easier to see texts as different kinds of objects.

Support for Discussion of a Text's Different Forms of Mediation

The rate of pure participation is only half of the picture. In review sessions dominated by reviewer contributions, writers had some difficulty steering the conversation to topics of interest to them. In other words, the more dominant participant chose how to think and talk about the reviewed text. In turn, that person set the agenda for the review. The participatory imbalance can result in a review that focuses on a text's organizational function while only indirectly discussing changes to the writer's practices.

Another way of framing the issue is that the balance of participation is an indication of the degree to which each participant's expertise or experience is allowed to shape the review. Balance is required in order for the reviewer to address a text's dual role in the maintenance of organizational culture (reviewer's experience) and the change/creation of it (writer's experience). The textual replay appeared to afford this balance and to allow the participants to initiate discussion of the text as an object of different mediational forms (i.e., as an object of organizational need and as an object mediating ongoing writing process).

In the text-mediated reviews, the reviewers frequently discussed rhetorical and organizational issues, but often indirectly. They would suggest that texts were connected to other texts or that other people in the organization may play some role in deciding what gets written. Often these comments were non-specific about their application to writing process. For instance, at the Donor Relations office, one reviewer offered these comments about a troublesome paragraph in a solicitation letter:

> **Reviewer:** I thought this paragraph was one that truly would have the potential to resonate particularly strong for a faculty. You link the goals of the [university mission statement] and the initiative to create an international reputation [. . .] It was really for that reason that I thought this one letter was in many respects sort of the outstanding letter of this group, and it had to do with how you brought together who you were and what you said to them, or that you caused the president to say to them (Donor, Callie, Text).

This comment sets rhetorical and process issues in a complementary relationship, connecting parts of the letter to the organizational needs that they serve. The letter works because it links the university mission statement with an initiative to raise the school's international profile. The reviewer commented that the donor officer was ghostwriting for the university's president, another connection to someone whose interests are served by the letter. It is unclear, however, *how* to link the mission statement with other initiatives. It is unclear what the writer can reasonably "cause" the president to say.

Likewise, other reviewer-initiated interchanges introduced issues of text appearance and rhetorical context by linking the text to a wider network of social motives. Reviewers would often ask about the text's genred form in order to suggest a mismatch between what was written and the social motives that the text would serve. These issues were infrequently connected to concrete writing practices. For example:

> **Reviewer:** Why do a press release?
> **Writer:** Well, you know because I think it's interesting that government, the neighborhoods and the school are getting together to try to improve the neighborhoods.
> **Reviewer:** Yes, but what is the idea of doing a press release? That they'll put this in the newspaper or that they'll come?
> **Writer:** That they'll come, yeah.
> **Reviewer:** So you'd really like to get a reporter to come and show up (Media, Gertrude, Text).

Although the review yields a discussion about the merits of a press release over a photo-op, the conversation started as a discussion of the press release and its organizational function. The conversation did move toward a discussion of the writer's intentions, but not before the reviewer insisted that the writer reconsider her use of a press release. Ultimately, the reviewer recognized that the press release was more appropriate, but not before talking to the writer about her intentions.

In the textual-replay-mediated reviews, the writers exerted more control over the direction of conversation. Their interchanges focused on process and text issues, for two reasons. First, the writers needed to explain the textual replays. Second, the writers raised discussion and asked questions relevant to their immediate task of writing and revising.

> **Writer:** And so I wanted to keep each emissions source separate, and then what I end up doing is I go back and start making little paragraphs describing each of the emissions.
> **Reviewer:** Right, because in a permit review report the emission unit description will comment on all of that (Engineering, Ezra, Textual Replay).

By initiating this conversation about process, the writer made a joint activity out of establishing his motivation. The reviewer responded by acknowledging the motivation and connecting it to his knowledge of an organizational activity that was connected to the text under review.

One effect of initiating conversation about writing practice is that, in those instances, the explanations, questions, revision suggestions, and counter-proposals that followed all connected to writing practice. For example, revisions were articulated in terms of strategies for carrying them out.

Whereas the imposition of rules for text development can lead to encultura-tion, greater writer control and participation leads to more opportunities for individuation. Reviewers still frequently suggested why the writers' ideas would not work, but the writers were able to articulate their viewpoints and attach them to a concrete representation of writing activity.

Support for Coordination of Intent and Need

The reviewers initiated interchanges about rhetorical and text issues and the writers initiated interchanges about process and text issues, but what makes these changes significant is that reviewers interacted with writers more often in textual-replay-mediated reviews. As a result of this coordination, review conversation was more likely to relate discussion of rhetorical and process information. For example, in the textual-replay-mediated sessions, writers who contributed comments about process were answered by reviewers, who offered complementary comments about rhetorical issues. As we saw in the previous review excerpt from the Engineering Agency, the writer's comments on his motivation for expanding discussion of the emissions sources was justified and reinforced by the reviewer's comments about the interconnection between related texts in the permit application process.

Another indication that coordination improved in textual-replay-mediated reviews was an increase in questions, coordination-building devices that the reviewers used to enhance their understanding of process and to prompt writers to consider revisions. The questions created scaffolding upon which the writers expanded their practices by coordinating them with the reviewer's (see Hutchins, 1995, pp. 281-282).

In the text-mediated reviews, reviewers asked questions infrequently. Consequently, there were few opportunities for the writers and reviewers to combine their experiences and jointly apply them to revisions. One explanation is that the reviewers *assumed* coordination; they assumed that the writers already understood and could appreciate the organizational constraints on their writing. A more likely explanation is that writing review did not require coordination to produce an effective text, so long as the writer followed revision directives.

If a review serves a gatekeeping function in which the reviewer determines if texts are ready for public use, then there is little explicit need for the reviewer to serve as a teacher. Assuming that effective writing is as free from rhetorical decision-making as this model suggests, an overly directive writing review is not necessarily problematic. Writing is not that simple, of course, as evidenced by the fact that experienced reviewers in a single organization frequently disagree with each other (see Bernhardt, 2003). The evidence of conflict among reviewers suggests that some coordination on issues of process is desirable, and should coordination be difficult to achieve, conflict may be an acceptable substitute.

In the textual replay condition, questions about all topics increased. The textual-replay-mediated sessions appeared to encourage questioning because they also created conditions that promoted joint engagement and participation in the review process. The largest increase came on questions about text and process issues, indicating that the availability of process information made it easier (and more important) for the participants to form those questions. In many cases, the writers also asked more questions about process, perhaps to prompt the reviewer to consider ways of enacting proposed revisions.

The text-mediated sessions did not produce much coordination. The reviewers had a clear idea of what the texts needed to accomplish and made revision suggestions accordingly. Throughout, reviewers made many revision suggestions, and in doing so indirectly pointed to contexts in which the texts were meaningful artifacts. The writers did not appear able to demonstrate a similarly rich understanding of their texts.

The textual-replay-mediated reviews produced far more coordination. In fact, as the data suggest, the textual-replay-mediated reviews created conditions in which the writers and reviewers became more coordinated on all issues, as the review warranted. The participants achieved the best coordination on issues of process and text.

Through the writers' contributions, textual-replay-mediated reviews focused strongly on process, especially on the writer's composing practices. With the focus on process, the reviewers were better able to articulate the need for revisions after building a shared understanding of the decision making behind the original. For instance:

> **Writer**: So do you think that reading the story that it's fair?
> **Reviewer**: It's fair.
> **Writer**: Okay. So that's why I put him there because I was like "he's guilty of these things" . . . "okay he's guilty of these things, but his father says . . ." You know, he admits these things. You know what I'm saying? And then I put *[person]* right after that, and the reason that I put that he was staying cool through the arbitrator's decision was because I . . . because *[person]* and *[a different person in the courtroom]* had such similar names. I did want people to realize that this was *[person]* talking and not the guy.
> **Reviewer**: Right
> **Writer**: But maybe it would be something to put *[person]* said
> **Reviewer**: Yeah, I just think that you give the guy "what the hell" . . . "what do you think about it" (*Metronews*, Kassandra, Textual Replay).

In this exchange, the writer explained how she arranged the quotations to create a fair portrait of the story's subject. The reviewer contributed by adding that the mayor's quote should also move because he was the public response. At this suggestion, the writer understood how the reviewer envisioned the story and how the story would be read. The reviewer coordinated with the writer by demonstrating an understanding of her motivation (to be fair) and by using that information to frame his revision suggestion. Without coordination on process, the reviewer's suggestion might not have been as effective.

Writers and reviewers link rhetorical and process information consistently in almost all of the textual-replay-mediated reviews (with only one exception in twelve reviews). In the text-mediated sessions, only 51.1% of interchanges with rhetorical information were linked with a discussion of process. In the textual-replay-mediated sessions, 73.6% of interchanges with rhetorical information were linked to discussions of process. For this reason, it is significant that the reviewer in the above example linked rhetorical information with the writer's intentions and writing processes. The reviewer spoke about how to move quotes, treating the story as an object under development. He also linked in rhetorical information about the news genre. The reviewer was speaking about writing process, moving the quote, but he was also linking that process to rhetorical motivation (the mayor is the "public" response).

In other cases, reviewers linked writers' practices with the social structure and cognitive architectures through which the text must pass:

Reviewer You interpreted your own thing, and I interpreted [person in donor office]. You guys are working with lots of myriad perceptions. Fear, you know, that's a big one. You know all of the people going out there on the annual fund and all of us realize that.

Writer: Right, there's a lot of holes there.

Reviewer: Right, there's some fear that maybe perhaps you will be asked to do more and yet on the other hand we can't jeopardize our highest institutions. We cannot for the good of the university. So, we need to point out that there are some issues.

Writer: Well, and I look at how I derive my own tier ones now. I fill those ranks out before and I think that of those 34, 16 or 17 or so are just reunion folks. So, I just say I've looked at it, and we have a "cash in" goal.

Reviewer: That sounds okay (Donor, Frank, Textual Replay).

These linkages could produce specific revisions, for example, "point out that there are some issues." At other times the link to rhetorical information came through talk about other texts:

Writer: I wanted to keep each emissions source separate, and then what I end up doing is I go back and start making little paragraphs describing each of the emissions sources.

Reviewer: Right, because in a permit review report, the emission unit description [a section of the report] will comment on all of that; however, which way do you want to take it?

Writer: Right

Reviewer: The process is—it will ask you separately for process descriptions and those will be separated out automatically.

Writer: Okay, well these are all one process, but they are different emissions sources under the same process.

Reviewer: Yeah, well they will separate the emissions sources (Engineering, Ezra, Textual Replay).

In this exchange, the writer explained how he selected the different processes to include. The reviewer linked that action with other texts and activities at the Engineering Agency.

Support for Creating a Medium of Joint Action

Coordination across all topics of discussion and especially coordination between rhetorical and process information offers evidence that the writers and reviewers shared perspectives about how to look at the text when they engaged it through textual replay mediation. Coordination indicates that the participants could talk to one another and that they both could engage the text on an equal footing. The writers and reviewers both possessed the ability to talk about the text in ways that were individually meaningful and mutually comprehensible.

Evidence of coordination suggests, then, that textual replay would create conditions for joint action in the verbal construction of the text as an organizational artifact and as an artifact of an ongoing writing process.

Writers certainly stand to gain from their interactions with more experienced writers; however, reviewers also stand to gain from their interactions with writers. By watching an inexperienced writer act on a set of goals and objectives, a reviewer can speculate about how goals and objectives may have changed. By hearing what motivates writers to compose as they do, reviewers can recognize if there is still sufficient organizational/contextual exigency to merit any changes or if changes are in order. In the former, the reviewer finds reasons for the writer to be a contributor to existing organizational culture, in the latter to become a maker of it.

A critical component to this review method is the availability of writing performance and a surface on which review participants can jointly enact revisions. Paper, shared files, electronic libraries, and databases all contribute to the impression that the texts they contain are fixed and stable artifacts. As a surface for joint action, the "finished" text invites a discussion of the design and the mediation that it provides. A textual replay, by contrast, disrupts a text's appearance by showing the stages of its construction. The stable and fixed form is still available, but the textual replay adds another dimension that makes it possible to look at both the fixed and fluid states of information.

If the only surface for joint action is the finished text, then the range of joint activity will be more constrained. A text does not easily bridge the gap between what writers and reviewers perceive to be their common ground. To the experienced reviewer, the text is an organizational artifact that, once released into the public sphere, will go on to serve some mediating purpose. The writer, who may lack a similarly rich awareness of a text's public life, will be more familiar with the writing process that brought it about. The perception gap will be most noticeable in terms of the revision suggestions offered.

The text-mediated sessions had more directive (i.e., rule-based, compulsory) revisions. Revisions came out as demands, compulsory changes that the writer was required to make in order to improve the text to meet unstated standards. Since the text-mediated reviews appeared to encourage reviewers to compare writers' texts to genred ideals, the reviewers seemed to perceive less of an urgent need to explain their revisions.

> **Reviewer:** "Well, when I reviewed this, my first comment was that the first paragraph needs to be titled 'background' . . . so I think that some of the information you provide up front should really be incorporated into the background" (Engineering, Willis, Text).

The reviewer's comments exemplify directive revision suggestions. First, the revisions assume the writer's understanding. It was difficult to tell why the first paragraph *needed* to be titled "background," and it was unclear why the information up front *should have been* incorporated into the background. Even assuming that the writer understood why the material *should have been* incorporated, we could not assume that he also understood what the reviewer meant by "incorporating." The reviewer had already considered how the text should have been changed and simply formulated those changes in his mind. All that remained was to tell the writer what changes to make.

Textual replay appeared to offer a slightly better mediation of joint activity. Undoubtedly, it was important for the reviewers to look at texts as objects to be released into the public sphere, but it was also important for them to talk to writers about practical concerns. The textual replay brought an element of writing performance back to the surface. More importantly, it took pieces of the reviewed text, which appeared static, and animated them, infused them with information about writing process that could only come from encountering the text in a different representational format.

Further, because the text was viewable through two different lenses, both the reviewer and the writer had expertise to contribute to the review. The revision then became a means of reconciling organizational need with the goal-oriented strategies that the writers brought to bear on their texts. Textual-replay-mediated reviews appeared to encourage this kind of joint perception and action.

The revisions offered in the textual replay reviews were more facilitative. Often the reviewers would make tentative suggestions, prompting the writers to offer their assessments about the suitability of the revisions and the fit between the suggested revisions and their intentions. For revisions that everyone agreed were needed, it appeared easier to work together toward their enactment.

> **Reviewer**: [B]ut if you know you have done a more complete job in the permit review report you might want the permit issued to show those more complete descriptions as well.
> **Writer**: Oh, I see.
> **Reviewer**: [S]o you might want to change that to put it in the application so that it displays it in the permit as well (Engineering, Ezra, Textual Replay).

Prior to this suggestion, the writer had discussed why he included so much detail about the emissions sources, information that the reviewer used in shaping his revision request. If the detailed emissions descriptions appeared in the permit review report, the writer might want to consider having the same level of detail in the permit. To achieve this consistency, the writer would need to include the emissions descriptions in the application. Permit review reports do not typically have such detailed explanation. The reviewer prompted the writer to explain the reason for such detail. Satisfied that the detail was important, the reviewer suggested that the writer keep it and also to put the same level of detail in other texts so that the emissions detail could circulate into other work activities.

The paper text did not show this emissions detail, because it had been removed by the time the text came up for review. Under text-mediated circumstances it is unlikely that the reviewer would have learned about the added detail, much less have read it. The writer's desire to add detail broke with the genre convention of providing less substantive detail, but the break with convention resulted in a more useful text that the reviewer was able to recognize. The reviewer acknowledged that the writer's inclination to provide more detail was a good writing practice. He then inflected that process-based knowledge with rhetorical information, noting both how the writing practice should be extended to other texts, but also by noting how other texts (i.e., the permit) could benefit from this expanded information. The review became an opportunity for individuation.

In the textual-replay-mediated sessions, the reviewers produced more facilitative suggestions, which treated writing as a cooperative project. The facilitative revision suggestions encouraged participation from the writers, who posed questions and raised challenges that forced the reviewers to explain their perceived need for revisions. The discussion of process appeared to elevate normally private decision-making to the level of a public performance in a way that we do not typically see.

Often when the reviewers proposed changes, they treated the texts as if they were under construction, allowing the review to become a public space in which changes were jointly negotiated and enacted. The review was then used to coordinate perspectives through the joint, participatory design of the text. For example:

> **Reviewer**: Now I don't—do people know what *[local business]* is?
> **Writer**: I mean, I think—this is going out to the general, and I think that they all know who *[local business]* is—I mean I have a background that explains it [. . .]
> **Reviewer**: I don't think you need to add . . . but you might say "*[local business]* a *[city]* based operation.
> **Writer**: Oh, okay, I will bring that up when I mention that it is *[city]* based.
> **Reviewer**: I don't think you need to move all of this up.
> **Writer**: No I don't think so . . .
> **Reviewer**: But so that people understand real quickly that . . . you know it could be that the *[local newspaper]* will just print this (Media, Gertrude, Textual Replay).

In this exchange, the writer and reviewer discussed possible additions to a press release, particularly whether or not to add background information on a local business that had partnered with the university. The writer challenged the reviewer's suggestion by noting that the general public would recognize the business. Realizing that the news outlets (the intermediaries between the media relations office and the general public) would first need to be convinced to run the story, the reviewer suggested that the addition of location would help the news outlets recognize the story's importance. In addressing the writer's challenge, the reviewer gave options for revision while still explaining their necessity ("you know it could be that the *[local newspaper]* will just print this.").

As the writer spoke of her writing practices, it became clearer to the reviewer that his revision suggestion needed explanation. His explanation prompted a more explicit and open discussion of the press release as a news artifact and of the most effective writing practice for creating one. The discussion here, like those elsewhere in the textual-replay-mediated sessions, built coordination between the writer's sense of text and the reviewer's enculturated sense of text, and then tied both to writing practices.

The increase in facilitative revision suggestions is one indication that the reviewers' and writers' cooperative interaction had a strong pedagogical component. The fruit of this pedagogical activity is, hopefully, coordination between the ways that the writers and reviewers see their texts. However, organizations differed on how facilitative or directive revisions became. In some organizations, texts were simply less negotiable because there was less that could have been changed.

THE NEED FOR SITE ANALYSIS

While there are some consistent differences between text-mediated and textual-replay-mediated writing review, the difference in technologies does not, alone, account for all of the variation among organizations. A more comprehensive explanation must take into account the people and the organizational culture as well. At some of the organizations (i.e., *Metronews*, Media Relations) employees recognized their principal work as "writing." In those settings, the reviewers were trained, professional writers. These are practice-oriented organizations, whose review practices, conventions, and environments are set up to accommodate reviews that focus on writing process. These reviewers and writers have less to benefit from textual replay because it is a technology that appears to support a discussion that they were already capable of sustaining.

Artifact-oriented organizations (i.e., Donor Relations, Engineering Agency) differed in that the employees' primary work was seen as something other than writing (e.g., engineering). This perspective was reflected in the practices, conventions, and environments for writing review. It was reflected in the fact that those who reviewed writing were not professional writers. Reviewers and writers in artifact-oriented organizations had more to benefit from the textual replay as it supported a kind of writing review that they might not otherwise have attempted or have seen as beneficial.

These organizations differed on other accounts as well—on the social and organizational lives that texts live, for instance. In artifact-oriented organizations, texts were more likely to become permanent, mediating artifacts with a broader scope of effect. In practice-oriented organizations, the effect was different. The strong focus on writing process overshadowed the more limited, but still substantive role, that their texts played as mediating artifacts, even if for shorter periods of time and with a more limited scope of effect. Chapter 6 and Chapter 7 address these differences, respectively.

CHAPTER 6

Textual Replays in Practice-Oriented Organizations

In practice-oriented organizations, textual-replay-mediated reviews were associated with

- greater writer participation,
- more facilitative revision suggestions, and
- better overall coordination.

Yet these outcomes cannot be solely attributed to the textual replay. Instead, the positive outcomes result from a new writing review dynamic facilitated by textual replay. Simple alterations to the material conditions of review can create situations where writers and reviewers are encouraged to interact differently and to achieve the goals of writing review through different means. For this reason, differences among organizations have some influence on the overall mediational impact of a technology like textual replay. The goal in this chapter is to talk about the impact of textual replay in practice-oriented organizations.

Writing reviews at *Metronews* and the media relations offices had two goals: to produce the best possible text and to teach the writers strategies for producing better writing in the future. Both goals require writers and reviewers to coordinate how they think about their texts, the writing practices that led to their creation, and organizational uses that are crystallized in the genred forms those texts take.

At *Metronews* and the media relations offices, writing reviews were generally positive experiences for the writers. The writers and reviewers were all trained writers who were comfortable talking about writing processes and ways to improve them. They worked in an organization that allowed greater individual variation in the texts writers produced. Most importantly, the writers and reviewers alike treated the review as an extension of the writing process. The organizational culture helped close the distance between what the writers and reviewers shared as common knowledge (see Figure 1).

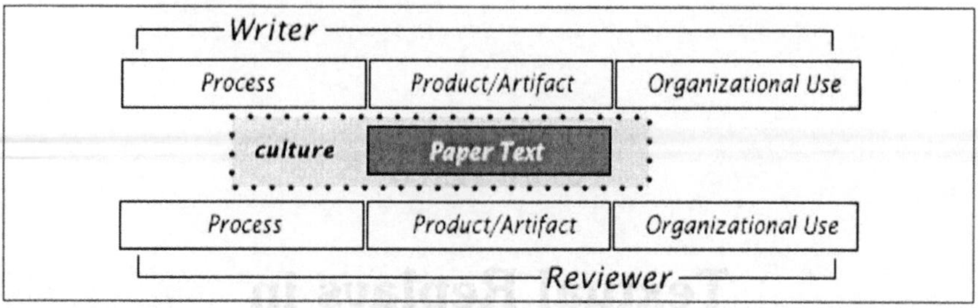

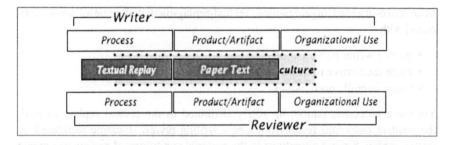

Figure 1. In a professional culture that values writing process,
common ground is partially extended to an understanding
of process and organizational uses.

Figure 2. Textual replay extends the mediating effect of culture
on issues related to writing process.

The writers and reviewers both shared a common professional orientation to writing and writing process issues. As a result, the textual replay duplicated some of the effort needed for coordination between writers and reviewers (see Figure 2).

However, on some measures of writer participation, facilitation, and coordination on writing process, the writers and reviewers did better in the textual-replay-mediated sessions, suggesting that the technology may serve some purpose in practice-oriented organizations.

SUPPORT FOR INTERACTIVE EXCHANGE
BETWEEN WRITERS

In the practice-oriented organizations, textual-replay mediation further enhanced the participants' ability to engage each other as writers. As trained writers, the writers and reviewers at *Metronews* and at the media relations offices were more comfortable talking about the design of a text and the writing processes underneath them. Because of this relationship, one might expect reviews in practice-oriented organizations to require less cognitive effort from the reviewers and writers to switch between talk about writing process and the genred form to which a text should adhere. The figures on writer/reviewer coordination in the text-mediated review support this assumption (Table 1).

Even without the assistance of textual replay, the writers and reviewers were nearly twice as likely to be initially coordinated on text and process issues. Moreover, the writers and reviewers were also more likely than their counterparts in artifact-oriented organizations to talk about process issues at all. Even when they were not talking about writing process, they were performing it.

> **Writer**: I don't think we've ever said it [place where shooting occurred].
> **Reviewer**: Got it, right.
> **Writer**: I call it [name of convenience mart].
> **Reviewer**: and it's really [neighborhood], 5th street market.
> **Writer**: No, if we do that it would be, "an" [neighborhood] - because …
> **Reviewer**: Okay, I don't mind that.
> **Writer**: Because it . . . "the" makes it seem like there is only one.
> **Reviewer**: Except it's "a convenience store."
> **Writer**: We've called it a neighborhood market, C—has. I thought that we took that out.
> **Reviewer**: I'm just saying is it "an" or "the."
> **Writer**: No, "an" means one of [neighborhood] neighborhood markets, Oh, after he walked.
> **Reviewer**: But, it's the second reference to this store.
> **Writer**: "outside of" oh, okay.
> **Reviewer**: No, we said convenience is "a."
> **Writer**: Okay. I would do "the neighborhood market in [neighborhood]."
> **Reviewer**: No, we said it happened outside of a convenience store. A gunman, . . . leaving an [neighborhood] store, so then it's there at the [neighborhood] neighborhood market.
> **Writer**: Yeah (*Metronews*, Tina, Text).

The writer did not hesitate much to offer revision suggestions of her own. This writer engaged her reviewer as if the review was an extension of the writing

Table 1. Practice-Oriented Organizations Had Greater
Initial Coordination on Process

	Media relations	Metronews	Donor relations	Engineering
Text	8.8%	28.5%	4.3%	13.4%
Process	8.8%	7.1%	4.3%	4.3%

process. They were, in fact, re-writing parts of the text as they reviewed it. Additionally, the immediate connection between discussing a writing process and seeing a revision helped solidify the connection between intent and outcome. Many of us would recognize this kind of interaction as a productive and cooperative exchange between writers. The writers and reviewers still disagreed, misunderstood each other, and revised the text toward conflicted ends. That is, some discoordination was still present, but the textual replay enhanced the positives by increasing the likelihood of coordination and by keeping the review discussion productive.

While the reviews at *Metronews* and the media relations offices came across as cooperative interactions between writers, their organizational function was still evaluative and supervisory. The reviewers still held responsibility for "approving" content and for "approving" a particular manner of expression. This kind of organizational responsibility does not always augur the kind of pedagogical outcomes one might expect in a review between like-minded writers. In the text-mediated reviews, reviewers appeared more reluctant to develop a text freely than they were in textual-replay-mediated reviews. In text-mediated review, the reviewers were more apt to assert control over a text's content and expression. In these reviews, an average of 71% of the revision suggestions were directive, changes the writers were required to make. Organizational responsibility aside, however, the writers and reviewers were still professional writers, and there was only so much direction that the writers needed. Although only 29% of the revision suggestions in it were facilitative, this percentage was still considerably higher than the 18% in artifact-oriented organizations.

In the textual-replay-mediated reviews, the percentage of facilitative revision suggestions increased to 65% (35% directive). The reviewers' organizational responsibilities remained constant, but the textual replay pointedly reminded them that the texts they reviewed were products of a writing process on which they could also comment. The reviewers did not give up the right to shape the reviewed texts, but they did open up more to discussion of process.

The push and pull of directive review practices was replaced by a subtler nudge and tug method. The reviewers encouraged the writers to assert their intentions and then pushed those ideas as far as they could go while making subtle corrections along the way to nudge the text back on course. In the following, for instance, the writer and reviewer dig in to the author's lede, both with ideas about how it should change.

> **Reviewer**: I just think that lede needs to be sharper, an "alleged rogue cop."
>
> **Writer**: The reason I used "rogue cop" is just because, *[person at *Metronews*]* . . . the last time my story ran he was saying 'we need to say he was a rogue cop' because people know him. We need to put that up high

because other than . . . there [are] people [who] are like 'who is [police officer]?'" And that's how he's been characterized before.

Reviewer: Alleged rogue cop. That definitely doesn't.

Writer: You don't want to [. . .] Well, I mean you call him rogue cop, [police officer], and it's almost like you yourself are judging him, that the writer is judging him.

Reviewer: Well, I'm not going to drop the "alleged" but of "21 charges the city filed against police officer, [police officer]" "only two weren't punishable according to" or I mean it is a state arbitrator has found, right? [. . .]

Writer: How about "of the 21 rogue cop charges," . . . no? [. . .] Considered [police officer] a rogue cop [. . .] Wanted [police officer].

Reviewer: wanted police officer [police officer].

Writer: You don't want to use "police officer," you want to use "rogue cop." So, I mean you just say . . .

Reviewer: Well you've got to say "police office [police officer]" fired, right?

Writer: But then the "rogue cop" where are you going to put that?

Reviewer: Considered [police officer] a rogue cop and wanted him fired, right? (*Metronews*, Diane, Textual Replay).

The writer originally drafted her lede to include the phrase "rogue cop." The reviewer wanted to soften the phrase to say "alleged rogue cop." The writer treated the review as an opportunity to explain her reasoning. The police officer in question had already been brought up on charges, making "rogue cop" appropriate, but blunt. The reviewer believed that the word "alleged" highlighted facts that made the story newsworthy for a different reason (i.e., the fact that some charges were pending). The reviewer could easily have required the writer to include the word "alleged," but instead allowed a back-and-forth exchange in which they mutually offered revisions, rejected them, and offered alternatives. The review was somewhat messier, but perhaps more pedagogical.

Arguably, one of the primary functions of writing review is to serve as what Prior (1998) called a "mangle of practice." The reviewers were figures invested with organizational and experiential authority. Writers submitted to reviewers their texts, which were to be "mangled" into shape. Under this pedagogical model, the writers would learn by submitting themselves to the wisdom of an authority. The alternative pedagogical model that started to take hold in the textual-replay-mediated reviews was more cooperative in nature. In those reviews, the division between the authoritative reviewer and the writer was less distinct, although not invisible. The clearest indication of this softening distinction was the increase in facilitative revision suggestions.

Although a positive sign, sharing ideas does not necessarily lead to understanding. A text-mediated review in one of the media relations offices offers a good example. The writer and reviewer debated the most appropriate way to describe a lighting demonstration that students would be hosting. The writer wished to include information about the purpose of the event and who would be in attendance. The reviewer wished to strike some of the information, suggesting that the writer produce a photo-op instead of a press release. Not until many conversational turns later did the writer indicate that she had included the information in order to suggest to the news outlet that they could get interviews. Rewriting the press release as a photo-op would hide this message. At this point, the reviewer recognized that the press release was the most appropriate form for the information. This pattern repeats itself. Comments that are rooted in coordinated understanding of the writers' processes developed into revision suggestions that were based on clear intentions, had clear effects, and were clearly actionable. The textual replay facilitated the movement of this process information from private (writing) space to the semi-public review space, where it could be more readily shared.

With a technological medium to facilitate discussion of process and text, the writers and reviewers improved their ability to coordinate on the same issues (see Table 2).

A portion of the cognitive effort involved in cooperation comes from participants shifting attention between various work objects (i.e., text as process and text as organizational artifact). When the work objects are abstract, linguistic constructs (as "writing process" would be in text-mediated review), the cognitive effort is greater and more energy must be expended ensuring that the writers and reviewers are thinking about issues in the same way.

In text-mediated review, the effort required to shift attention away from the stable draft text to writing process would be substantial. The participants would need to create a linguistic representation of writing process that they both understood equally well, enough to make changes to it. Even among the most like-minded colleagues, the ability to understand and manipulate virtual objects like these is unevenly distributed.

Textual replay relieves some of the burden of achieving coordination by making concrete what was once abstract. There is less chance for equivocal interpretations of how a paragraph developed if there is a tangible record of its creation. By making writing process partially visible, writers do make their

Table 2. Coordination on Issues Related to Features of Textual
Appearance and Writing Process Increased in
Textual-Replay-Mediated Reviews

	Media relations		Metronews	
	Text	Textual replay	Text	Textual replay
Text	3.0%	13.6%	14.9%	33.3%
Process	2.4%	14.6%	3.2%	17.6%

actions vulnerable to misinterpretation. It is not always clear what will happen when a textual replay enters the review space. Certainly there is potential to abuse the textual replay, for reviewers to jump to the conclusion that the amount of text a writer produced can be divided by the amount of time it took to produce, as a measure of efficiency. However, this kind of outcome would depend on the social and organizational environment.

Review space at *Metronews* and at the media relations offices was not so strictly evaluative. Review was an opportunity to extend writing space. In this kind of environment, the textual replay was not treated as an object of evaluation. Rather, it became a platform for sustainable cooperation. As we see in the following, a writer's articulation of motivations and intentions often led to a more mutually acceptable revision suggestions.

> **Writer**: Yeah, I mean the one thing that I don't want to do in this story—is although I have their side and I'm saying some good things about them—the fact that his wife is a teacher and he is popular. *I don't want to make it seem like I'm on their side.* I mean . . .
> **Reviewer**: Right.
> **Writer**: *So do you think that reading the story it's fair?*
> **Reviewer**: It's fair.
> **Writer**: Okay. So that's why I put him there because I was like "he's guilt of these things" okay, he's guilty of these things, [. . .] and then, what was I going to say you—and we're kind off the track, but last time you were like when *[person at Metronews]** was looking at this that "we don't want to mention that his father was a legislator." Should we mention that anywhere in the story? That he is a legislator?
> **Reviewer**: Uhm, yes we can probably mention it where we mention that his wife is a teacher.
> **Writer**: Okay.
> **Reviewer**: because he is a respected guy in the community. His father is a legislator.
> **Writer**: Okay (*Metronews*, Diane, Textual Replay—my emphasis).

It is telling that the reviewer spent some of his time trying to understand the writer's motivations (i.e., to be fair) and used that discussion to talk about how to arrange information to enhance the text's ethos of impartiality. In this case, revision became more cooperative because the writer and reviewer arrived at a common understanding of the intentions that informed the piece.

SUPPORT FOR VIEWING TEXT AS AN OBJECT OF A WRITING PROCESS

Eventually, a reviewed text will become an artifact that circulates through different organizational and professional contexts. Before it reaches that stage, the text must first be an object that mediates the writer's ongoing writing process.

The textual replay helped portray the reviewed texts as objects whose current form was the result of specific writing and revision practices. Ostensibly, part of the purpose for writing review is to shape the text in such a way that it successfully mediates a continuing writing process. To fulfill this purpose, the writers and reviewers must have some way of looking at the text as a particle in a stream of other texts that are created, overwritten, and discarded in the course of a writing process.

The textual replay afforded this unique way to look at the text, as a series of snapshots in time and as a stream of writing activity. Each textual replay is comprised of hundreds of successive screen shots laid out on a timeline that approximates the amount of writing activity that took place on screen. At any point in that timeline, users can view what a section of text looked like at that moment—a particle view. The users could also see "real time" writing, words appearing and disappearing—a stream view of text. Each view prompted different kinds of discussion. Talk about the text as particle emphasized its status as an organizational artifact. Talk about the text as a stream of writing activity emphasized the process by which it took shape. When viewing a text as a stream of activity, for example, one journalist talked about her writing as a process situated in the present tense, something that was ongoing and on which she prompted the reviewer to participate.

> **Writer**: This was, obviously, one of my pensive moments. I was—I wanted to actually get a sense because I felt that this man being sick and basically for the doctor's note not being allowed to face his maker and go to court. *I want to give the parallel to sort of a student kind of in school being excused from class because they have a doctor's note.* So I'm trying to find a way to say that this (*Metronews*, Tina, Textual Replay—my emphasis).

The textual replay showed how the writer had been working and reworking the lede in order to draw out the parallel that she hoped for. At this point in the review, the writer had not pushed her text to a point where she felt comfortable calling it done. She did not say, "I *wanted* to give the parallel" she said, "I *want* to give the parallel." I prefer not to think of the present tense as a slip, but rather as an invitation for the reviewer to take part in crafting the lede. The textual replay reinforced the sense that this text was in a state of development and that the current iteration of the lede was a step in that process. This perspective also allowed the reviewer to see where the text was headed and how to get it there. The reviewer could then choose to assist in that process or alter it. Similar cases occur in the media relations offices as well.

Narration of the writing event stream often created a context of activity out of which the reviewer could understand how the writers' motives intersected with the outcome present in the reviewed text. In many cases, the information revealed through the textual replay created a firmer basis for writer and reviewer to cooperate. The information increased the likelihood that the writers and reviewers would share a common understanding of what motivated the writer to start.

In the particle mode, the writers could present portions of their texts at different moments in time. They could take those moments and state what the text was doing. By stopping the textual replay at a certain point in the stream of writing activity, the writers asked the reviewers to turn attention away from the unfolding activity and direct it toward the textual product again. This textual product, however, may only exist in the past. Figure 3 illustrates how the textual replay was used to such an end.

The writer started the textual replay by skipping ahead to the lede she had written at 14:00 minutes into the writing session. Before playing out the rest of the textual replay, she noted that her intention was to give a balanced report:

> **Writer**: Yeah, I mean the one thing that I don't want to do in this story—is although I have their side and I'm saying some good things about them—the fact that his wife is a teacher and he is popular—I don't want to make it seem like I'm on their side (*Metronews*, Diane, Textual Replay).

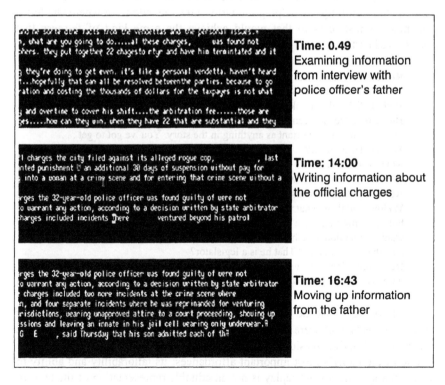

Figure 3. Segments of a textual replay showing a writer's drafting.

As shown at this moment in time, the lede reflected what the writer considered to be a fair representation of the story. The point of showing the lede appeared to be connected to the writer's comments that followed, in which she recruited the reviewer's assistance in adjusting the lede to be fair in the manner that she had stated. Her narration of the events shown in the textual replay indicates the process that she used.

> **Writer**: Okay. So that's why I put him there because I was like "he's guilty of these things" "okay, he's guilty of these things, but his father says . . ." You know, he admits these things . . . you know what I'm saying? And then I put [police officer] right after that, and the reason that I put that he was staying cool through the arbitrator's decision was because I . . . because [police officer's father] and [police officer] had such similar names I did want people to realize that this was [police officer] talking not the guy.
> **Reviewer**: Right.
> **Writer**: But maybe it would be something to put [police officer] . . . said . . . (*Metronews*, Diane, Textual Replay).

With a complete version of the lede to evaluate, the reviewer could then participate in drafting, by helping the writer take the lede from where she left it and make adjustments to that would achieve the same kind of fairness that she showed earlier.

> **Reviewer**: Yeah, I just think that you give the guy . . . "what the hell . . ." "What do you think about it."
> **Writer**: What do I think about?
> **Reviewer**: No, I mean what do you, meaning the defendant think about his . . . is this as important as anything in the story. You've got to get . . .
> **Writer**: Him higher?
> **Reviewer**: his response immediately.
> **Writer**: And then you want to put the mayor up higher saying that . . .
> **Reviewer**: Yeah because he's the public response to it.
> **Writer**: and then, what was I going to say you—and we're kind off the track, but last time you were like when J___ was looking at this that "we don't want to mention that his father was a legislator" should we mention that anywhere in the story? That he is a legislator?
> **Reviewer**: Uhm, yes we can probably mention it where we mention that his wife is a teacher (*Metronews*, Diane, Textual Replay).

There are signs that the textual-replay-mediated reviews led to discussion of texts as objects that were under negotiation. Yet it is surprising that in the text-mediated review sessions the writers and reviewers did not take advantage of one of the paper's most important affordances: its tailorability and ability to accept marks. The textual replay is not an editable representation of the text. In order to carry out revisions inspired by looking at the textual replay, the review participants needed to go back to the text. The reason why the participants did not use the text in this way from the start could be that viewing the textual replay helped make the paper text *seem* more negotiable.

The textual replay allowed the writing review to focus on not only what the text should become, but also on how it should get to that point and how this process of emergence coincided with the writer's intentions. Reviewers and writers looked at reporting, drafting, formatting, and revision. As a result, the review discussions were more richly infused with talk about writing process, which appeared to coincide with an increased number of revisions (see Table 3).

Viewed alongside the decrease in directive revision suggestions and the increase in facilitative suggestions, the increased discussion of process and more frequent revising indicates that the review participants were considering a wider range of revision options. In other words, the writers and reviewers did more work together and revised the text more extensively. That many of these revision suggestions came out as strategies was also an indication that the revisions could be applied to the reviewed text and others like it. In this sense, the paper text was treated more as an object that would mediate the writer's future writing activity. Only in the textual-replay-mediated sessions did the paper texts appear to become more malleable in this way. The writers and reviewers treated the papers as surfaces on which different revision strategies and ideas could be both experimented with and recorded in such a way that they could mediate the writer's next draft.

The text's surface had already been a medium for coordinating ideas about how well the text served its function and how it could be revised to do so more effectively. Now the writers and reviewers treated the text as a surface for holding information that the writer would later use on another draft. To facilitate this work, the writers and reviewers marked the review texts with additional information. For example, see Figure 4.

As the writers and reviewers looked at the paper texts, they discussed the writing processes that shaped them, and drew attention to the professional and organizational circumstances that ought to constrain their development. The reviewers added marks to the page that indicated such information. The reviewer wanted to indicate where to move sections of text. As the writer described what she had written, the reviewer determined how sections of the article hung together. Sections of the text that supplied information about previous court

Table 3. The Number of Revisions Offered Increased in the Textual-Replay-Mediated Reviews

	Media relations	Metronews
Text-mediated review	107 (35.7 avg.)	233 (77.7 avg.)
Textual-replay-mediated review	149 (49.7 avg.)	278 (92.7 avg.)

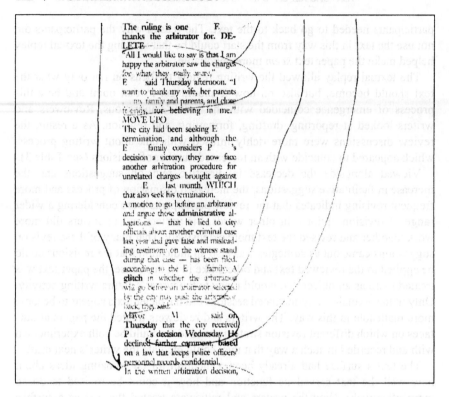

The ruling is one E.
thanks the arbitrator for. DE-
LETE

"All I would like to say is that I am
happy the arbitrator saw the charges
for what they really were,"
E   said Thursday afternoon. "I
want to thank my wife, her parents
    my family and parents, and close
friends, for believing in me."
MOVE UP O
The city had been seeking E.
termination, and although the
E   family considers P   's
decision a victory, they now face
another arbitration procedure for
unrelated charges brought against
E   last month. WHICH
that also seek his termination.
A motion to go before an arbitrator
and argue those **administrative** al-
legations — that he lied to city
officials about another criminal case
last year and gave false and mislead-
ing testimony on the witness stand
during that case — has been filed,
according to the E   family. A
glitch in whether the arbitration
will go before an arbitrator selected
by the city may push the arbitrator
back, they said.
Mayor   M   said on
Thursday that the city received
P   's decision Wednesday. He
declined further comment, based
on a law that keeps police officers'
personnel records confidential.
In the written arbitration decision,

**Figure 4. Markings on paper text that leave a trace of the
thinking behind revisions.**

cases became the "background information." The reviewer circled these sections and moved them further back on the page. Information that the writer included to illustrate the story's importance was labeled part of the introduction and moved back.

The markings may not appear different from the editorial marks that reviewers might make in any other situation. The difference is in the conversational context. The writer and reviewer discussed intent and motivation and then negotiated where to move chunks of text based on the purposes they served. The snapshot of activity above (Figure 4) represents a process of negotiating changes and thinking about a text—information the writer could use to guide her future revision. The text now carried additional meaning, reflecting the writer's and reviewer's experiences, which they layered onto the text (see Swarts, 2004a). The added layers of information enrich the text's function as a cognitive artifact. The paper captured part of the process by which those views were expressed, negotiated and substantiated as revision suggestions.

In its own way, the paper approximated the stream and particle perspectives. In the stream of review activity, the text was transformed through the markings that appeared on the page. The text was an object under development. Then, at some point, the review reached a resolution and the review participants agreed on a new vision of what the text could become; the text was frozen at this stage as a particle—the marked text. The marks only stand in as instructions for changes. They mediate the text's semantic potential.

While the reviewers did allow the writers to explore the limits of their writing intentions, they also made good on their responsibility to talk about a text's organizational and professional obligations. The reviewers examined the writers' texts in terms of how they were developing into artifacts that would serve useful purposes in various professional and organizational contexts. Although the textual replay did not provide much information about contexts, textual-replay-mediated reviews were associated with an increase in the amount of discussion about rhetorical and text issues (see Table 4).

However, as we saw in a previous example, without also connecting this contextual information to a discussion of a writing process, there would be limited opportunity for the contextual information to mediate a writer's composing process.

Although the textual replay does not reveal information about use context in any tangible way, there is some indication that the reviewers used them to talk about such issues. Perhaps, as the writers' intentions became clearer, potential conflict with organizational and professional uses likewise became more apparent. While the writers at *Metronews* and at the media relations offices produced texts that were more flexible and open to interpretation, they were still based on recognizable genres that revealed something of the discursive actions that they served.

The news story genre starts with a lede. Journalists recognize that newspaper readers are likely to scan headlines and read only the first few lines of a story to decide if it merits further attention. The lede, then, must capture the essential news, portray the relevant facts, and set the context that makes the facts newsworthy. These needs are reflected in a fairly familiar genred form.

Table 4. Rhetorical Information was Increasingly Associated with Comments about Textual Issues

	Media relations		Metronews	
	Text	Textual replay	Text	Textual replay
Rhetorical	3.0%	13.6%	14.9%	33.3%
Rhetorical + Textual	2.4%	14.6%	3.2%	17.6%

Similarly, press releases have recognizable structures. As one writer put it, the essential qualities of the press release are to cover the 5 W's: who, what, where, when, and why. These genred features are also a concession to busy readers in a newsroom. Unless the media relations writer highlights the important facts and emphasizes a story's newsworthiness, it may not be picked up. The media relations writers must also be aware if the release will be published "as is," a possibility that may compel them to include enough information that the release could stand on its own.

While the amount of rhetorical discussion did increase and was increasingly associated with specific demands on the text's appearance, the discussion was often too lean or imprecise to yield specific revisions. For instance, the following exchange showed how the reviewer implied the kind of change the text would need, but did not clearly specify a strategy by which the changes could be applied, nor was there a clear motivation or intention that the writer could dispute.

> **Reviewer:** [S]o we are assuming that everyone that reads this understands what a web server is.
> **Writer:** I hope so. Yeah. I would think that that is a fairly common thing around here.
> **Reviewer:** Well, you admitted yourself that you were not too sure what a web server is.
> **Writer:** Well, that's . . . that is my understanding. I haven't questioned my understanding of what a web server is, but . . .
> **Reviewer:** I kind of question if people even know what a web server is, but I . . . when you are writing for [campus publication] I think that is . . . it is fairly safe to assume that those people who read [it] will know what a web server is. But it is one of the sort of terms that I think we should explain . . . explain what exactly the thing is, especially since this is all about this guy creating a web server (Media Relations, Petra, Text).

In this example, the reviewer tied rhetorical information (audience and publication forum) to very specific revisions, but not to revision strategies. The trouble with such revision suggestions is that they do not help establish common ground between what the reviewers know about contexts and what the writers know about them.

The reviewers continued to give hints about the contexts in which reviewed texts would be used, but often that information showed up only as talk about a text's features. The reviewers may have been facilitative about asking for revisions, but to leave these revision suggestions at the level of changes in form is not likely to result in the writers forming concrete strategies.

SUPPORT FOR LEARNING BY DOING

The pedagogical interactions supported by textual replay fostered joint action between the writers and reviewers. *The textual replay helped create a review dynamic in which the writers worked with the reviewers instead of submitting to their authority.* The reviewers begin to pass on their experiential and enculturated knowledge by guiding writers' composing activities. The writers, on the other hand, create conditions in which the reviewers can reflect on their enculturated assumptions about writing and determine if they apply. For review to foster joint action, two conditions must be met: writing process must be elevated to the level of public performance, and the writing review must become an opportunity to revise the text and not simply pass on instructions for changes.

The most visible outward effect of textual replay is that it makes writing practice a visible phenomenon. Increases in the amount of conversation about process and increases in writer participation are the chief indicators that writing process has become a more accessible object of study. From the standpoint of the argument developed in this book, a publicized writing practice would appear to be a positive outcome. Yet in looking at the activity captured by the screen capture program, one might develop the impression that some messy aspects of the writing process are best left hidden. Occasionally, the textual replay revealed notes, poorly formed sentences, and very long pauses, for example. Once recorded, however, these practices become part of the review. In the right kind of review setting, however, these warts and blemishes can help reveal problems and create a solid basis for joint action. This level of disclosure leads to better over-the-shoulder learning experiences.

In one writer's case, the textual replay showed a great deal more about her writing than she had intended. While writing about the research partnership, the writer started to assemble quotes about the impact of the center on the local economy (see Figure 5).

The textual replay then captured her inventing a quote for a state senator (see Figure 6).

It also revealed her making changes to a quote from the university president (see Figure 7).

It turns out that both quotes were placeholders, but were indicative of the kinds of quotes that the writer both hoped and anticipated she would get.

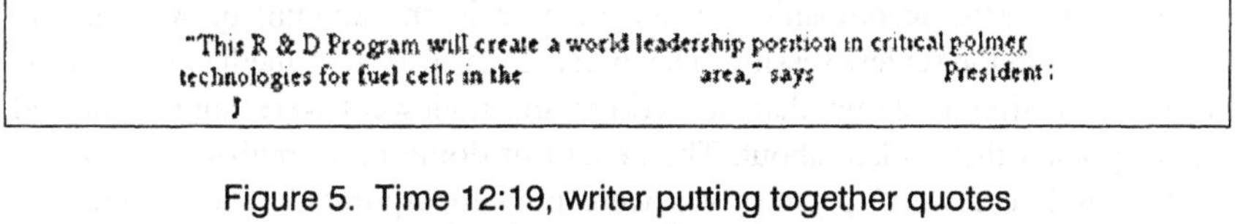

"The Center for   is ready to leverage its expertise and facilities polymer science to lead the development and testing of critical polymer technolog necessary for fuel-cell research," says B   , director of the polymer c

"This R & D Program will create a world leadership position in critical polmer technologies for fuel cells in the   area," says   President :
J

Figure 5. Time 12:19, writer putting together quotes
about a research center.

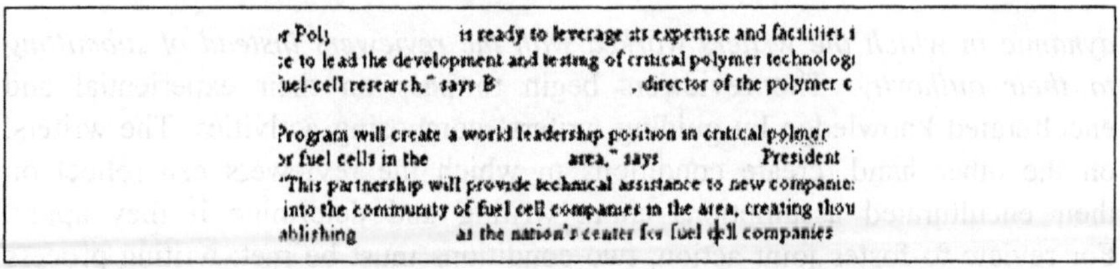

> r Pol; is ready to leverage its expertise and facilities i
> :e to lead the development and testing of critical polymer technologi
> 'uel-cell research," says B , director of the polymer c
>
> Program will create a world leadership position in critical polmer
> or fuel cells in the area," says President
> 'This partnership will provide technical assistance to new companie:
> into the community of fuel cell companies in the area, creating thou
> ablishing as the nation's center for fuel cell companies

Figure 6. Time 13:30, writer fabricating a quote for a state senator.

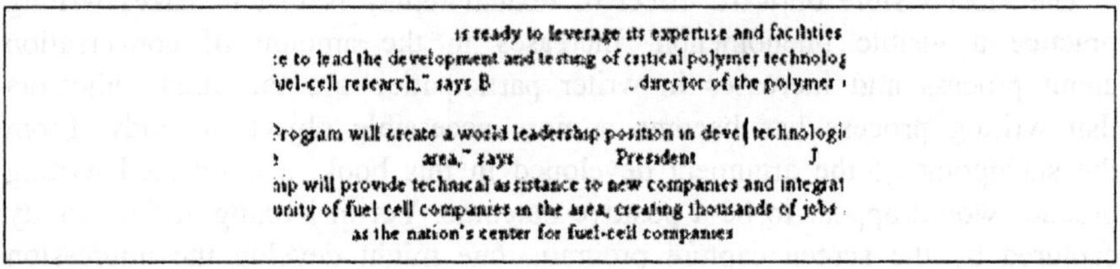

> is ready to leverage its expertise and facilities
> :e to lead the development and testing of critical polymer technolog
> 'uel-cell research." says B . director of the polymer .
>
> Program will create a world leadership position in deve [technologii
> : area," says President J
> nip will provide technical assistance to new companies and integral
> unity of fuel cell companies in the area, creating thousands of jobs .
> as the nation's center for fuel-cell companies

Figure 7. Time 13:50, writer changing the quotation from
the university president.

The benefit of this accidental disclosure is that it provided a spark for conversation about ways to make the press release work better. The reviewer ended up suggesting that the writer's inclination to focus on "jobs" in the senator's "quote" would be a good angle to play up in the press release generally. The reviewer and writer even came to agreement on the most specific way to achieve this goal.

The difference between seeing such an accidental disclosure as positive or negative depends largely on how the review situation is constructed. If the elements are in place to make the writing review a cooperative, pedagogical experience, then gaffes like this will have happened in a safe place where they can be put to productive and not punitive ends.

The presence of both process and rhetorical information, as we saw in the example above, is positive in that it suggests that the writers and reviewers were drawing on two relevant sources of information for writing effective texts. Further, by vocalizing this information, the review participants shared information in a way that could be applied specifically to revision. These shifts in conversation were accompanied by an increase in the amount of writing and revising during the review session. The increase (over the text-mediated sessions) in revisions offered shows that the writers and reviewers were digging in and applying what they talked about. The benefit of doing more revision is that the writers' and reviewers' perspectives were both incorporated. The writers and reviewers literally and figuratively guided each other's hands during the review.

When the writers and reviewers disagreed about a revision, those disagreements were communicated as both disagreements in principle and in practice. The following exchange illustrates the point.

> **Reviewer**: Let's maybe look at this from the standpoint of . . . certainly I think that what you were trying to accomplish through this particular paragraph, I think that you have done that successfully. I would, some of the other comments that you made, would though be something that needs to be worked in because what we want to do with this is not only to simply present the facts of the situation that he is coming here for this lecture, but also how fortunate we are to have this sort of renowned scholar, and if this is the first . . .
> **Writer**: since his ability is unique . . .
> **Reviewer**: yes—he is internationally . . . so maybe some background work is this is the first in depth book on this . . . on this person. And if it has won any awards, or if it has been . . . we will make it—we will package it really much more on a 'this guy really knows what he is talking about, and he is here at [college].
> **Writer**: Well sort of the narrower the niche, the more chances we can use those as a drawing point?
> **Reviewer**: Well, I think not necessarily narrower the niche. I mean that is certainly part of it too—what is distinctive about his work? But how well known is he? Personally, I had not heard of the guy.
> **Writer**: Yes.
> **Reviewer**: So if in this lede, you know, you might take a look at the "author of the first major historical perspective on the personality of Ho Chi Min and his place in history will be under discussion during the [lecture series]" (Media, Ben, Textual Replay).

Additional context will help clarify what this review segment shows. Just prior to this point in the review, the writer had expressed his interest in describing the lecture in such a way as to draw interest from non-academic audiences. The reviewer added information about the organizational work that the press release must do—it needed to suggest why the college was fortunate to have this speaker. Together, the writer and reviewer engaged the text and attempted to find ways to enact those changes. The writer suggested narrowing the scope of the audience he was trying to reach. The reviewer rejected this revision suggestion and offered one of her own—to revise the lede.

Exchanges like the one above and like the back-and-forth exchanges between writers and reviewers at *Metronews* depended on a review situation that encouraged such productive cooperation. To do so, the participants needed to see it as a pedagogical exchange, one where the more experienced reviewers guided the writers' actions, but also allowed them to experiment, venture guesses, and make mistakes. If we look at the conditions necessary to achieve such a review, we can see how the organizational context for review in practice-oriented organizations fit well. Together with paper text, the textual replay contributed to a cognitive architecture of review that met the following conditions. It provided:

- A shared understanding of performance that the review text represented;
- An artifact that held information about previous writing performance;
- An artifact that supported joint revision;
- An artifact that held a tangible record of the fruits of cooperation; and
- An artifact that retained a memory of the process that led to a successful revision.

When combined with the paper text, the textual replay met many of these requirements. The textual replay held an indexible and shareable record of writing performance. To the textual replay the writers and reviewers could offload the cognitive effort of explaining why a text looked as it did. They could also offload responsibility for talking about motivations and intentions. With the process information that the textual replay helped bring to the surface, the review space could become an extension of writing space. When the writers and reviewers did not need to exert as much effort to achieve a common understanding of intentions, motivation, and organizational obligations, they could spend more time enacting changes that they agreed on.

The textual-replay-mediated sessions were associated with far more facilitative and cooperative revision. The reviewers spent less time saying what needed to be done and more time asking the writers to consider the value of the revisions they had suggested. In other words, the reviewers started to treat the review as an opportunity to experiment with different revisions. As the review participants became more comfortable talking about issues of process, it was apparently easier for them to use that information to formulate revision strategies. The writers also started to offer more of their own revision suggestions. The reviewers did not always agree with the changes, but the disagreements were instructive, because they nearly always led to discussions about the merits of each proposed revision.

In the text-mediated reviews, the writers offered fewer revisions than their reviewers. At the media relations offices, the writers offered one revision suggestion for every 9.7 offered by their reviewers. In the textual-replay-mediated sessions, the writers nearly doubled their participation, offering one revision for every 5.4 by the reviewers. At *Metronews*, the ratios were closer. In the text-mediated sessions, the writers offered one revision suggestion for every 1.8 by the reviewers. In the textual-replay-mediated sessions, the writers offered one for every 1.4 offered by the reviewers.

The writers' suggestions arose out of a discussion of motives and intentions, helping link together writing performance held in the textual replay with revisions to carry the text forward.

Reviewer: Can we do something like that and get to the state funded program?
Writer: Sure, the state funded programs are recorded. . . . Sure, I mean is that too long a sentence, can we just use state funded program? Oh, I see "will be headquartered in" okay. How about "it will be in partner-ship . . . ?"
Reviewer: Yeah, make two sentences. That's a good idea because it's a long sentence.
Writer: I will—I will figure out a way to get another sentence (Media, Jessica, Textual Replay).

In this segment, the reviewer pointed out that it was not clear who was partnering with whom. The reviewer made an implicit claim that news outlets in the region would only find this press release newsworthy if they found information suggesting its importance to their readers.

The reviewer combined his understanding of the university's interests (publicize the good things that the university does) with what he understood to be the forces that would motivate news outlets to pick up press releases or to pass on them. He used this knowledge to guide the writer's revisions. The writer suggested including the language that the research center would be "partnered with" a local company, and the reviewer ratified that revision, affirming that the addition of local business names would meet the organizational and professional demands on the release.

The writers also took more risks by making more comments about their texts, asking questions, and making inquiries about the writing process. We can see these interactions as the writers' attempts both to understand their texts as their reviewers did, but also to steer how the reviewers were thinking about the texts.

The reviewers, likewise, also asked many more questions in the textual-replay-mediated writing review sessions. There were nearly twice as many questions in both the media relations offices (8.6 on average in the text-mediated sessions compared to 16.3 on average in the textual-replay-mediated sessions) and at *Metronews* (26.7 in text-mediated review and 49.3 in textual-replay-mediated review). Like the writers, the reviewer's questions were very often intended to clarify a different way of thinking about texts. The reviewers asked questions in a great variety of circumstances, but frequently asked questions to help writers think about ways to develop or organize content (e.g., "is there any sense of this guy as a ridiculous figure that we can get up higher?" or "Now, why not end the sentence there?"). In addition, when the writers and reviewers made interpretations and suggestions that appeared incorrect, misguided, or that would lead the text in a different direction from where it should go, the participants offered corrections to redirect the discussion or to make adjustments.

While the textual replay did offset the cognitive effort required for the writers and reviewers to achieve a common understanding of writing process, it had a much less significant impact on supporting a shared writer/reviewer understanding of organizational and professional contexts of use. Yet under the right organizational circumstances, the textual replay did appear to have an indirect effect on the effort that reviewers were willing to expend to make contextual circumstances clearer. This is the subject of the next chapter.

CHAPTER 7

Textual Replay in Artifact-Oriented Organizations

At Donor Relations and at the Engineering Agency, the settings for writing review differed significantly from those at *Metronews* and at the media relations offices. Where reviews at the latter were encouraged by professional, social, organizational, and technological factors that promoted a focus on writing process reviews, at Donor Relations and at the Engineering Agency, focused on evaluation. Despite the initial differences, writing reviews at Donor Relations and the Engineering Agency started to resemble those at *Metronews* and the media relations offices once textual replay was introduced. At the artifact-oriented organizations, textual-replay mediation was associated with:

- more writer participation,
- more writer-initiated interchanges that focused on writing process,
- a balance of facilitative and directive revision suggestions,
- better coordination on issues of text and process
- complementary coordination in which writers raised issues related to writing process that the reviewers connected to related rhetorical/organizational issues.

Donor Relations and the Engineering Agency are examples of organizations that focus on texts and their mediating functions as opposed to their origins as products of a writing process. This orientation influenced the nature of writing reviews in those settings. Vested with organizational authority to approve a text's content and expression, reviewers used the writing review to shape the writers' texts outright. Often, the result was an acceptable text, but the writers did not gather much specific information to use in guiding their writing practices from that point forward. The reviews separated the textual product from the writing process, leading to a review that only indirectly addressed questions about how to write within an organizational setting. Consequently, writers in these artifact-oriented organizations were only marginally better prepared to engage in the writing tasks that were increasingly a part of their day-to-day work.

A number of factors helped shape reviews at Donor Relations and the Engineering Agency as supervisory and evaluative rather than cooperative and pedagogical. These factors contribute to a writing review that encourages encul-turation at the expense of individuation. Individuation is still a goal, however, because it is through that process that newcomers learn to see connections between their actions and what their colleagues consider literate and conse-quential contributions to organizational streams of activity (see Katz, 1998; Winsor, 1996). To get writers to this point, reviewers must look at texts as artifacts that will ultimately mediate organizational work and writing processes. To do so, writers and reviewers must find ways to recognize and overcome inertial professional, organizational, and technological forces that suppress talk about writing process and encourage reviewers to exert tremendous control over the development of a writer's text.

The first issue is to address concerns how to overcome the writers' alienation from their own texts. Many of the writers at Donor Relations and the Engineering Agency did not consider writing to be their primary professional responsibility. These writers frequently produced anonymous texts, ghostwrote, or only con-tributed to texts. They had a constrained sense of ownership over their texts. The "particle" view of text during review, reinforced by the static presentation of paper text, appeared to encourage the writers and reviewers to treat reviewed texts as artifacts and to disavow concerns about the text as an object of a writing process. The sum effect was less talk about writing process and fewer oppor-tunities to connect information about what the text should do to the ways writers can make them do that work.

To many of these professionals, writing was a byproduct of their interactions with technologies, people, and information. The engineers, for example, visited businesses that were applying for permits, and these encounters typically resulted in a variety of texts, including field reports, permit applications, and study protocols. Similarly, the donor officers interacted with donors and university officials, interactions that resulted in solicitation letters, contracts, and proposals. To many of these writers (and their reviewers) the texts were means to ends. Neither the reviewers nor the writers appeared to give much attention to the writing processes by which the work that they considered important was enacted.

A second factor concerned the reviewers' situated authority. The writers and reviewers felt a strong sense that the texts they produced belonged to the organizations for which they worked. As representatives of their organizations, the reviewers were expected to exercise control over the texts' content and expression. They appeared predisposed to favor "particle" views of text, which emphasized the text's appearance.

The tangible effect of this writer/reviewer dynamic was that the writing review became more evaluative and less facilitative. Further, the reviewers appeared to interpret their roles as gatekeepers, whose function was to modify texts prior to their release into organizational work streams. This function appeared not to include cooperative, joint revision, by which their experiential understanding of writing might be better communicated.

With textual replay, the reviews started to resemble those at practice-oriented organizations. The reviews focused more on writing process. They were more attentive to aspects of the writer's context, and they were less rigidly determined by the demands of organizational need. Unlike the reviews at practice-oriented organizations, the reviews at Donor Relations and the Engineering Agency remained focused on artifactual concerns. The way in which these artifactual concerns remained, created a unique context for talking about writing process.

SUPPORT FOR A TWO-WAY LEARNING EXPERIENCE

Unlike the writers at *Metronews* and at the media relations offices, those at Donor Relations and the Engineering Agency entered into a review after they considered their texts to be finished. Also unlike their counterparts, they did not appear to treat the review as an extension of the writing process, but rather as an opportunity for evaluation. The reviewers, too, approached the review in the same spirit. Consequently, there was significantly less writer input about process and intended revisions. The writers participated to some extent, but usually by offering information about the text's content. The resulting review dynamic was a one-way learning experience in which the reviewers passed on what they knew about the text's function, unfortunately in sometimes vague and abstract ways that were unconnected to a writing process. *In the textual-replay-mediated condition, writers and reviewers appeared to learn from each other.*

There are signs in the text-mediated reviews that the reviewers asserted a high degree of control over the writers' texts. Reviewers contributed most of the conversation, and spent much of that time talking about what writers needed to change. The little discussion that concerned writing process frequently came out as the reviewers' imperatives about what the writers needed to change and how.

The reviewers frequently talked about organizational knowledge, indirectly describing the mingling of organizational exigencies and their collective influence on the reviewed text. The reviewers also referenced this rhetorical information, which stemmed from their lived experience, as a way of justifying changes. Lacking the same experience, the writers had limited access to that rhetorical knowledge base. The results were often review conversations primarily dominated by reviewer contributions. In one Donor Relations review, for example, a writer presented a contract, the purpose of which was to stipulate the terms of a donor's gift of stocks. Drawing on her knowledge of the university's interests and legal requirements for processing such a donation, the reviewer asked for very specific changes in the contract's overall organization.

> **Reviewer**: All right, I would say, if I was this person taking a look at this . . . a couple of things. Second paragraph was obviously a disclaimer.
> **Writer**: Right.
> **Reviewer**: That protects [university], correct?
> **Writer**: Right, we are not engaged in doing any illegal stuff.
> **Reviewer**: Definitely, and I think that needs to come up pretty far (Donor, Ivan, Text).

Underlying this comment is the reviewer's awareness of the disclaimer's importance. The reviewer recognizes the contract's organizational function and translates that motive into a directive change to move the disclaimer up. The writer's intentions are beside the point, because the text is intended to serve a legal function, which it did by taking on the form that the reviewer had specified. To the writer, the change may have seemed appropriate, but perhaps not clearly warranted. In this case, as in others, knowledge moved primarily in one direction: from the reviewer to the writer. Unfortunately, this case is also similar to others in that the underlying motivations were not always clear.

The writers were at a disadvantage to connect information about organizational processes to their writing and revision processes. The language of organizational process was the reviewers', and it was based on inaccessible experience that set discussion of the texts at an abstract, organizational level. For example:

> **Reviewer**: Well, I'm going to leave the methodology of how you get the sample and the integrity of the sample up to you. You just need to verify with the lab that the method you use is attemptable and that it is foolproof in case we ever had testing audit. That is what I expect you to do (Engineering, Simon, Text).

The engineer tried to decide on the most appropriate and current sampling techniques to include in his study protocol. His motivation, we find out later, was to describe accurately the sampling techniques and to choose techniques that would most likely result in hard data. The reviewer directed attention to the organizational level, shaping the text by reference to the work stream of lab technicians. His aim was to make changes in the study protocol that would cover any potential liability concerns. To the reviewer, "hard data" was a slightly different phenomenon. The specifics of his experiential understanding and its bearing on future revision was left noticeably under-specified. The reviewer passed up the opportunity to discuss how to think about sampling techniques in terms of their integrity and how to describe the techniques so that the lab received foolproof samples:

> **Reviewer**: [s]o we are talking strategy and I am assuming that the method-ology that you use will have been thought out and corroborated by whoever is going to do the actual analysis. So that is a question of chain of custody or handling (Engineering, Simon, Text).

The text was left stranded at a level of organizational abstraction in which the engineer's writing and revision processes were tied to a "chain of custody" and to a list of people who needed to corroborate the protocol. A couple of effects associated with comments like these merit specific attention.

First, these kinds of comments make it appear that texts supported static work practices that are rigidly governed in a top-down manner by organizational processes. Second, the comments suggest that the reviewed texts could be legiti-mately evaluated against a genred ideal. The reviewers set the agenda for the writing review and their concerns about the future uses of a reviewed text directed attention away from the more immediate functions that the texts would serve to mediate the writers' revisions. Furthermore, such review practices directed attention away from the important connection between the act of writing and the act of literate, consequential participation in organizational work activities. Not surprisingly, conversation in text-mediated review was least coordinated overall, on both process issues (2.5% coordinated at Donor Relations, 1.7% at the Engineering Agency) and rhetorical issues (2.8% and 3.4% coordination, respectively).

For writing review to accomplish its goal of enculturation and individuation, there must be some opportunity for the writers to make the connection between organizational need and specific writing practices by which those needs can be met. The writers will not make these connections on their own. The reviewers must assist; however, the reviewers also need assistance bringing issues related to writing process closer to the surface of the review and closer to their conscious, articulate thinking. In other words, for the writing review to become more of a pedagogical experience, communication must be two-way, especially since reviewers will require the writers to assist them in refocusing on writing process. Textual replay helps achieve this bridge of clarity and joint participation. The textual replay raises process to a more prominent level and provides a concrete representation as well.

An immediate effect of the textual replay was increased writer participation. As the writers started to assert themselves, they began to steer the conversation back to points related to writing and revision. The shift in the participation dynamic can be partly accounted for by the writers' need to explain the textual replays. The increased conversation had a positive effect.

The writers brought to the review another mediating device that assisted them in retrieving information about writing process. While the reviewers had previously been concerned with texts' broader mediating functions, they had overlooked the fact that the text also mediated the writer's own writing process. The writers started to push conversation onto these process issues. For example:

> **Writer**: "I would like to present to—" I kept reading that, shortening that because she [the donor] doesn't want to read about all of this. I wanted to get right to the point.
> **Reviewer**: Of course, you would not need to write that second sentence and then this last sentence because they say essentially the same thing. Maybe you just decided that yourself? (Donor, Linda, Textual Replay).

By explaining the textual replay, the writer made that section of the text meaningful as a representation of her motivations (e.g., "I wanted to get right to the point") and as a representation of her writing strategy (e.g., "When I see that there is a particular style . . . I try to follow it"). This kind of writer participation introduces a language of process to the review. The writers created a different platform on which potential revisions needed to be articulated and justified. The writers also raised the potential for airing conflict between organizational and individual literate practices, creating situations for instruction and coordination.

The organizational processes still retained their importance and prominence, yet by raising issues of writing process, the writers created new opportunities for participation from the reviewer. The reviewer in the last example took the opportunity to voice her request for changes via a discussion of the writer's intentions. The reviewer referenced organizational information indirectly, noting that solicitation letters are courteous in that they are direct and to the point about asking for a donation. The reviewer also tied that organizational restriction to the writer's actions (e.g., "maybe you just decided that"). The reviewer did not say what to do, but instead appeared to speculate about what the writer might be thinking, thereby helping to structure the writer's interpretation of the events in the textual replay and, ideally, her revisions from that point on.

Increases in the amount of talk about writing process were not always accompanied by increases in rhetorical information from the reviewers. Even so, the type of rhetorical information introduced and the placement of that rhetorical information suggests that the conversation supported by the textual replay created conditions in which rhetorical information could be threaded together with process information. The number of process comments that were connected with textual comments in the same interchange rose between the text and textual-replay-mediated sessions (see Table 1).

With issues of writing process in the foreground, the reviewers often found a way to talk about those practices in terms of their organizational fit. As we see in the excerpt below, the reviewer's comments draw "writing" and "participation" in

Table 1. The Writer/Reviewer Coordination on Issues of Writing
Process Increased in the Textual-Replay-Mediated Sessions

	Donor Relations	Engineering Agency
Process with text	2.5%	1.7%
Process with textual replay	7.6%	10.3%

the organization together, a little more tightly. As a result, the writer learns how his motivations fit with what was expected of him.

> **Writer**: You know I had the very free, general "Weigh Tank A"—you know "Reactor Condenser A," "which is to condense, return [. . .] as chemical and then stop" and like Condenser A which does stop. And I was like okay, those are good, I guess like initial statements, but I was thinking . . . again not really knowing what to expect. I decided that I should really add in some more text to describe each of the processes that occur at that emission source.
> **Reviewer**: Yep.
> **Writer**: And that is kind of what I do next. So then I have like . . .
> **Reviewer**: Well, that is good. Because you are looking at this—you have to look at this from the standpoint of somebody that doesn't—of somebody that is not familiar with this facility.
> **Writer**: Right.
> **Reviewer**: The more descriptive you are, you know, the better it is for the non-technical person who is reading this like the public. Or even the EPA.
> **Writer**: Right, right (Engineering, Dennis, Textual Replay).

This conversation follows from the writer's narration of the textual replay. The reviewer joined the discussion of this process by talking about the writer's decision to include additional detail about the equipment configuration. The reviewer also contextualized the process by providing a rationale that was grounded in his understanding of the organizational work the text would do (i.e., "look at this from the standpoint of somebody that [. . .] is not familiar with this facility"). The reviewer learned what would motivate a person to write with the level of detail that this writer had done. As we find out later, the amount of detail was not typical for the genre, but the writer's explanation brought out enough information that the reviewer recognized the value of the change.

SUPPORT FOR COOPERATIVE RATHER THAN COERCIVE PRACTICE

With the writers participating more regularly, contributing more, and initiating more of the interchanges with talk about writing process, the participation dynamic started to change in other ways. *In the textual-replay-mediated condition, the reviewers exerted less control over the ultimate shape of the text and the writers exerted more control.* The writers started to make clear that they had stakes in the review process, in so far as they needed to make revisions and would, in the future, be required to produce similar texts. As the writers started to contribute more, they took more risks, offered more tentative revisions, and took guesses in ways that strengthened the reviews' pedagogical orientation.

An important factor in this change of review practice was the amount of talk about writing process. Typically, the reviewers had limited awareness of the writing processes that might have resulted in a recognizable, genred text acquiring an unexpected form. In one instance, an engineer produced a study protocol and in the objectives included language suggesting that the purpose of the study was to find known emissions violations. While the purpose of the study may have been to locate the emissions violations suggested in the site report, the reviewer indicated that they "don't want to indicate that there is a problem" before they actually conducted the tests. The reviewer's comments were based on his awareness of the ethos that the protocol must foster. Instead of getting at the reason why the engineer had worded the objectives as he had done, the suggestions for changing them came out as a directive. This action was instigated by the paper text, which presented the protocol as a designed artifact rather than as a series of partially finished ideas.

Reviewers appeared to base many of their comments on their enculturated genre knowledge, which magnified the problems talking to writers about writing process. As a type of technology, genres simplify writing by preserving ways of articulating and formatting information as conventions (Miller, 1984; Swales, 1990). Over time, the reviewers had become so familiar with the formal features of common genres that they lost an articulate sense of the discursive and social action that they supported. When the writers accessed these genres in the form of old, model texts, they may not have recognized the genre features that were the most important. The text spurs recognition of the presence or absence of genre conventions, but without information about writing process, the connection to a person's enactment of those social and discursive actions through writing was more difficult to reconstruct. Such was certainly the case in text-mediated reviews.

Increased emphasis on the formal features of genres as a measuring stick for evaluation suppressed issues that might reveal a conflict between the writers' intentions and the social motives served by a genre. Conflict, in this case, is a desirable starting point for building a learning environment. By addressing the conflict, writers could learn about the forces that ought to shape their intentions. Additionally, the reviewers could gain some critical distance from the genres that they implicitly recognize but may have lost the ability to examine dispassionately. Paper text reinforced a "particle" view of writing and appeared to encourage the reviewers to rely on their genre-based knowledge when assessing the content and manner of expression. Textual replay, on the other hand, appeared to help create productive tension by giving writing process a concrete form that required discussion to clarify.

Further, the reviewers' willingness to rely on descriptions of genre features helped create a dynamic in the text-mediated review where the revisions suggestions were far more directive. At Donor Relations, for instance, the directive revision suggestions outnumbered the facilitative 5.7 to 1. At the Engineering Agency, the disparity was similar at a ratio of 4.3 to 1. Often, these suggestions came across as imperatives:

> **Reviewer**: So, what to do. Well, first of all you have to do the business of the letter and you have to thank, you have to mention allocation, and you have to mention reunion where appropriate (Donor, Linda, Text).

From this excerpt, we can tell that the donor officer had little choice about the content of her solicitation letter. The reviewer clearly stated that the officer had to do the business of the letter, had to thank, and had to mention allocation and reunion. This letter, like many others, was a promotional and persuasive text. It spoke about campus events, created a rapport with the donor, and served as an informal contract. In this sense, the reviewer was correct to say that the letter had to contain the elements that she requested. These necessities, though, are clearly based on the function of an ideal solicitation letter and had little to do with the writer's situated intentions. Also absent from this discussion was any mention of the social or organizational motives supported by a letter with those features, or any discussion pertaining to the specific donor file on which the writer was working. Not only was the revision suggestion direct and imperative, it was non-specific and difficult to apply.

Even in situations where the reviewers did reveal information about relevant organizational circumstances, the extent to which that information ought to be applied was not always certain.

> **Reviewer**: Well, what I understand about [person at the agency], if you don't have costs ahead of time, you won't get the go-ahead for proposals.
> **Engineer**: . . . So I don't know if I should suggest that we don't really know what the cost would be. I mean I could try to get information, but the thing is that it is going to take time to get that information.
> **Reviewer**: . . . We can get estimates, and we might even be able to say that we are working on this portion of the costs (Engineering, Bill, Text).

The bottom line was that the cost information needed to be included or else the text would stall in the approval process. Ultimately, the timely advancement of the revision through channels of approval was more important, because it ensured that regulatory actions taken elsewhere would have legal justification. The engineer's concerns, though, were quite understandable. As the person responsible for the revision, he appeared reluctant to include cost information he knew to be incomplete. Was it better to include the incomplete information or to leave it out? At the end of this segment of review, we only know that the cost information must be included, no matter how incomplete. How does this information regulate future writing? Is it always better to go with uncertain information rather than no information?

One explanation for why revisions in the text-mediated sessions were directive is that they relied on fixed organizational circumstances. These situations *required* changes that the reviewers recognized by observing the absence of information or inconsistencies in presentation. Surprisingly, the reviewers infrequently mentioned rhetorical information in the same interchanges that they made and explained their revision requests (see Table 2).

While the reviewers may have created a broad rhetorical context, this information did not share a proximal relationship to the revisions that they entailed. One would need to question the writers' ability to make the connections on their own. In the following example, the rhetorical justification for a revision is unclear.

> Reviewer: What we will probably do is see what the secretary is saying. Okay they would know what is actually the proper way.
> Writer: Yes.
> Reviewer: Reading through here. I just thought was a little vague— "portions" is pretty vague as well. Some of them up there . . . would be a way to make it less . . . make it a little bit more clear.
> Writer: Okay.
> Reviewer: You still have to spell everything out I guess. This is all the strong stuff there a . . . and this is all [inaudible] stuff there.
> Writer: This is pretty much the same though the sentence is just a little different.
> Reviewer: This is all right. Oh, this wasn't (Engineering, Bill, Text).

Regarding the regulation's wording, the reviewer indirectly refers to a government official (the secretary) who was responsible for setting the exact wording.

Table 2. The Number of Revision Interchanges Associated with Rhetorical Content is Notably Lower than One Might Expect

	Text	Rhetorical	Content	Process
Donor Relations	39.9%	20.0%	21.5%	41.7%
Engineering Agency	60.9%	33.3%	49.3%	69.6%

This reference was a good start, but when it came to making changes, the reviewer was less clear about the demands that this context placed on the text. He noted that the engineer would need to be clearer about the word "portions," without specifying the kind of clarity needed.

Among all of the directive revision suggestions, many were associated with discussion of process, meaning that the reviewers directed how the text should be changed without talking about how or why to bring about the changes. These revisions came out as comments like, "[s]o you need to meet with S___ or whoever the manufacturer of these units are. That is the kind of information you need to extract." The writers were frequently told what to do, with enough specificity that the texts in question would be suitably revised. Whether the writers could apply such revisions forward to future texts, remained unclear. Further, we do not know how the writer envisioned the application of this revision and do not know if the writer's interpretation was in conflict with the reviewer's intentions.

More generally, the reviewers' tendency to dictate process seemed to indicate that the writers were not expected to have different ideas. Potential conflict between what the writers intended and what was expected of them appeared to be treated as moot points. Yet, this is the kind of conflict that we want to encourage, because it creates fertile grounds for future coordination.

A related issue is that the presence of directive revision suggestions indicates that the writing review was reinforced as an evaluative and supervisory practice. When review operated primarily for these purposes, enculturation was the result, but perhaps the more insidious, narrowly-focused kind of enculturation where the writers learned to produce the genres, but failed to see reasons why. Genres do not change without some outside force pushing on them, and if the writing review cannot be the place where this conflict is unveiled and exerted, then faulty writing practices and outmoded genres are likely to persist far past the point that they continue to serve a useful purpose.

The textual-replay-mediated reviews were conducted in ways that encouraged a productive, pedagogical conflict. The reviewers offered more facilitative revision suggestions. When the revisions were presented as options, the writers had the opportunity to evaluate, accept, or reject them. They also gained the opportunity to interpret the revision suggestions and speculate about different ways to enact them. Both outcomes showed that the writers and reviewers started to treat the review as a site for cooperation, that the writers were more willing to voice their opinions, and that the reviewers were more willing to listen.

Under these conditions, writing is not only made into a relevant issue, it becomes a performance elevated to public space, where it can be more directly guided by the reviewer's experience-based knowledge. Moreover, the more visible profile of the writing process is associated with more precise information about how writers could carry out the revisions asked of them. This alone is an improvement. By pushing writing performance, motivation, and intention to the surface, textual replay helped make conflict more visible. It helped to dramatize the potential mismatch between actions and expectations. What ideally follows from such writer disclosure is cooperation on writing practice.

The textual replay drew attention to writing and revision as important contexts in which the writer was, and would be, working. The paper text acquired additional importance in this situation, as an artifact that mediated the revision. The paper text became a site for coordinating revision practices with the reviewers' experiential knowledge. Paper texts also acquired more prominent status as artifacts that would mediate a writing process in the distant future, as model texts. Under these circumstances, different issues were at stake—not just the shape of the reviewed text, but also the shape of the writer's approach to the writing process.

The increase in facilitative revision suggestions indicates that the reviewers were doing more to enlist the writers' assistance in articulating, approving, and operationalizing a course of revision. For example, at the request of a colleague, a donor relations officer tried to incorporate two themes into a solicitation letter and remarked, "Well, this is kind of a theme that I took from the annual fund piece, and [person] wanted an incorporation of the two ideas [...] This is kind of what she wanted to do with it."

The reviewer responded, "It seems to me that you might be able to say something like 'donors to the [university] annual fund constitute a powerful community,'" picking up on one of the themes that the writer was pursuing (i.e., the strong character and influence of the donor community). However the reviewer pitched her suggestion more tentatively (i.e., "you might be able to say"), inviting the writer to compare the suggestion with her intentions. This move drew out information about the writer's approach so that it, too, became a subject of discussion.

The writer's inclination to take the letter in a different direction from other letters became evident through her narration of the writing process. The reviewer expressed some reservation over the original wording, but on hearing the writer's rationale, offered revisions that kept with the writer's intentions, testing how far she would be willing to adjust the language. Would the writer accept a revision that the donor was a member of "a powerful community" rather than "the most powerful community"? The writer used the opportunity to explain why she included the information, making an implicit case to adjust the tone. The resulting revision was a compromise, one that led to a change in the way the writer and the reviewer thought about the letter.

The facilitative revision suggestions created opportunities for the writers to move their writing practice into the public sphere where it could create pedagogical opportunities. Even if the reviewers knew the revisions that they wanted, it was important for them to witness how the writers arrived, or failed to arrive, at those revisions on their own. What the reviewers may have perceived to be problems may actually have been important indicators of how either a genre needed to be altered or the writer's sense of purpose needed attention. Another encouraging but somewhat unexpected finding is that the writers started to assert more authority over their texts. They started to make more of their own revision suggestions. They also started to ask the reviewers questions and to correct the reviewers' mistaken interpretations of their writing process (see Table 3).

We can see the increase in questions and corrections as a sign that the writers were becoming more engaged in the review process. We can also see this kind of participation as a sign that the writers sought coordination with their reviewers. The increase in questions and corrections may also help to explain why coordination on process and text-related issues rose in textual-replay-mediated review. Yet what makes this outcome surprising is that the writers appeared to be treating the writing review less as a supervisory or evaluative practice despite the fact that their disclosure about writing practice extended the scope of that supervision and evaluation.

In addition to offering tentative revision suggestions, reviewers frequently bundled suggestions with comments about the organizational processes in which the writers participated. By couching suggestions in discussions about organizational activities, the reviewers appeared to connect the writers' motivations and intentions to organizational exigencies that their texts ought to address.

Writer: We will take a look at—particularly at our example and compare and contrast it with the others, and then we will perhaps identify some of the dysfunction as you and I have talked about it here. And hopefully start to lead those discussions to kind of highlight what worked well.
Reviewer: I see, yeah, because I think as soon as you can put out the idea or even the thought of these more controversial—at least you can get people to react and hopefully get to a solution. Is that what you are after? Because what I would like to see happen is that we are—we are collaborative enough and trusting enough that during this particular session we can come out with some real ideas (Donor, Ivan, Textual Replay).

Table 3. The Number of Questions and Corrections Increases
in the Textual Replay, Indicating More of a Need to
Coordinate Thought and Action

		Questions	Corrections
Text mediation	Donor Relations	17.3 (4.2%)	5.0 (1.4%)
	Engineering Agency	9.3 (4.6%)	7.3 (4.0%)
Textual-replay mediation	Donor Relations	27.7 (7.2%)	15.3 (4.1%)
	Engineering Agency	24.7 (6.1%)	11.3 (4.4%)

The reviewer's revision suggestions were both directive and facilitative. The reviewer suggested that the writer's discussion of the "dysfunction" and the ideas for improvement were important, considering the purpose of the text. The reviewer proposed that "put[ting] the ideas" out earlier would be preferable based on her understanding of what the writer wanted to accomplish (i.e., "Is that what you are after?"). Although the revision suggestion appeared tentative, it really was not. Such suggestions were typical. Often phrased as questions, these revision suggestions invited writers to explore revision options under the reviewers' watchful eyes. In excerpt quoted above, the reviewer was seeking to uncover conflict and to work with it to guide the writer's hands to a more successful revision. This approach is preferable because it draws out writer motivation so that it can be shaped alongside the text itself.

This combination of directive and facilitative revision suggestions is somewhat unique to the artifact-oriented organizations. While the textual-replay-mediated reviews were more facilitative, they still retained a level of directiveness. The explanation can be traced to the functions that texts served in those organizations, functions that were more fixed and static in nature. When texts are expected to do very specific work, then there are fewer revision options available. Surprisingly, these demands were sometimes suspended in order for the writers and reviewers to talk about revision possibilities.

SUPPORT FOR COORDINATION THROUGH CONTEXTUALIZATION

While the textual replay helped create conditions that made review more like those in the practice-oriented organizations, the realities of writing review at Donor Relations and the Engineering Agency could not be overlooked. Texts were required to perform very specific mediating work, and for that reason they were required to contain very specific kinds of information, often expressed in prescribed ways. *Coordination on issues of writing process increased, but this information was tempered by a discussion of constraining rhetorical circumstances.*

Information about the organizational circumstances was just as obscured as the writers' knowledge of their writing processes. Organizational context is a very complex mediating factor, one that the reviewers saw quite clearly, but only acknowledged indirectly. Even when reviewers did talk about organizational circumstances, those comments were infrequently linked to discussion of writing strategies, practices, or motivations. Although the issues were important, the reviewers had few options for creating common ground with their writers about these issues. The textual replay did not *appear* to offer any assistance, but it did help. The writers and reviewers created a coordinated understanding of writing process by putting those processes within a larger organizational context.

The role of the textual replay was similar to one it played in practice-oriented organizations. At *Metronews* and the media relations offices, the textual replay provided information about writing practice. It revealed writing activity so that it became a fixed, articulated point around which coordinated and cooperative revision could arise. At Donor Relations and at the Engineering Agency, writing activity was taken up as an object of evaluation and as a point for coordinating revision.

In text-mediated writing reviews, the writers' knowledge of process and the reviewers' knowledge of organizational activity came into contact, but rarely in a way that they could be coordinated. Writers and their reviewers approached the reviewed texts from very different standpoints. The result was a notable lack of coordination in the ways that the participants discussed the text (see Figure 1).

The writers and reviewers were most coordinated when they spoke about the content of the reviewed texts (15.9% of interchanges were coordinated). On interchanges about rhetorical issues, the writers and reviewers were coordinated 9.9% of the time. On text and process, coordination was lower, at 7.5% and 4.5%, respectively. The low coordination on text and process is the principal concern, because these issues do the most work to contextualize a text in a stream of revision and organizational activity.

The textual-replay-mediated sessions showed an interesting change. First, the amount of process-related issues that writers introduced increased dramatically. Second, the amount of coordination between writers and reviewers increased uniformly on all content issues (Figure 2).

Coordination on text issues increased most dramatically, going from 7.5% coordination in the text-mediated sessions to 24.4% coordination with textual replay. Rhetoric (20.8% coordinated), content (25.8% coordinated) and process (14.0% coordinated) all showed similar levels of increased coordination. Importantly, coordination improved on those issues to which the writers and

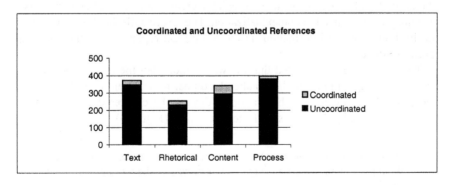

Figure 1. The amount of coordination in text-mediated sessions was low.

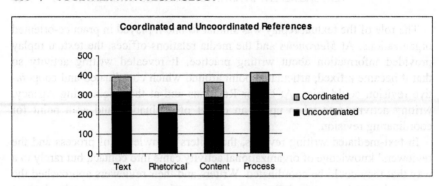

Figure 2. Coordination in all areas of discussion content improved
in the textual-replay-mediated sessions.

reviewers previously had limited joint access: process and rhetorical issues. Together, they started talking about tangible effects on the text.

The general increase in coordination aside, it is also important to note the increase in one type of complementary topical relationship. When writers or reviewers discussed process-related issues, the conversation was increasingly associated with talk about rhetorical circumstances (Table 4).

This finding suggests that even in situations where the writers and reviewers did not coordinate their discussion, they did introduce complementary subjects that connected writing practices to their organizational contexts. However, it is worth asking why a technology that raises process information to a more concrete form would also contribute to an increase in talk about information that it does not show.

As more process information entered the review, the information appeared to increase the writers' and reviewers' awareness that the text was incomplete and subject to changes that would be influenced by the writers' sense of purpose and direction. In other words, the textual replay increased awareness that there was a writing process in need of contextualization. The screen stills that follow will help to illustrate how the information raised in a textual replay could, and did, help draw out rhetorical information.

To start, the reviewer noted that the writer addressed the letter's recipient in an unusual way—imploring her to attend a dinner to be given in her honor. The writer used the reviewer's observation to discuss the choices that she made in the letter. Narrating the events of the textual replay (Figure 3).

> **Writer**: I was thinking about how she would react when she saw this letter. Would she think "hey, I already know that, why is she writing that in the letter"?
> **Reviewer**: Good point.

Table 4. The Number of Statements about Rhetorical Information that are
Accompanied by a Discussion of Writing Process Increase
in the Textual-Replay-Mediated Sessions

	Donor Relations	Engineering Agency
Text-mediated	55.1%	41.9%
Textual-replay-mediated	69.1%	65.3%

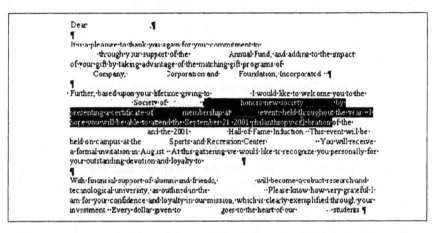

Figure 3. Writer is shortening sentences in the solicitation
letter [time: 13:57].

Writer: "I would like to present to—" I kept reading that, shortening that
because she doesn't want to read about all of this. I wanted to get right to the point.

The conversation started to get richer as the writer and reviewer attempted to
coordinate talk about process and rhetoric. The reviewer started to interpret the
composing activity that she was witnessing by attributing motives to the writer
(Figure 4).

Reviewer: Of course, you would not need to write that second sentence and
then this last sentence because they say essentially the same thing. Maybe
you just decided that yourself? Oh, you did.
Writer: I was thinking the same thing.
Reviewer: Yeah, this is kind of fun to watch it change before your very eyes.
"To recognize your outstanding devotion . . ." that is even better. Yep, fewer
words is better, right? Usually.
Writer: Hmmm "personally" I must have looked at another letter—I deleted
that paragraph in the first letter (Donor, Linda, Textual Replay).

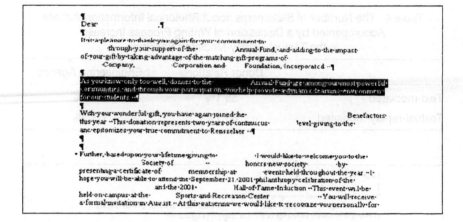

Figure 4. The reviewer offers an interpretation of onscreen
activity [time: 16:00].

The textual replay helped turn the writing process into an object for discussion and interpretation. It reinforced the perception that the words on the page were part of a stream of activity in which the writer operated from the motivation to be concise and knowledgeable while still accomplishing the business of the letter. The reviewer addressed these motivations by tying them to the rhetorical purpose of such a letter, creating a point of common ground that distributed the writer's motivations over organizational circumstances that ought to influence them.

By talking about writing process, in many cases, the reviewers became better at talking about the impact of organizational factors. They started linking information about context to concrete writing practices and to specific ways that the reviewed texts could and should be revised. The kinds of rhetorical information discussed varied and pointed to the ways that texts mediated an organization's work. The first kind of rhetorical information concerned the localized and individualized work practices supported by the texts. Very often the reviewers mentioned specific people in the organization and the work that they would do with the text.

At Donor Relations, one writer was charged with writing a report about reunion organization. The point of the text was to spur conversation about other schools' approaches, but it was not until the writer had gone through his textual replay to elaborate his purpose that the reviewer was able to link changes in his composing practices to the kind of outcome that the text was designed to bring about.

At other times, the reviewers switched between discussions of individual and organizational processes, showing how they connected:

Reviewer: Okay, I understand what you are doing.

Engineer: But I should have the technical information to back that up?

Reviewer: It would be nice that if somebody comes up and asks why you were removing that or why you want to make all of the other ones have this—you need to be able to show that it makes no difference in there anyway.

Engineer: Right and that was one of the questions that I was going to ask the manager at [[contractor]] if that was cancelled, because I couldn't find it.

Reviewer: Okay, it is just nice to have that in your back pocket in case somebody asks (Engineering, Brad, Textual Replay).

Although the reviewer understood why the engineer made the deletion (i.e., because that section made "no difference" anyway), he exhibited an awareness of how others in the organization might react. The reviewer suggested that because people in the Engineering Agency might not understand the reason for the omission, as clearly as the engineer who made it, he ought to consider including technical information in other sections that could be used to justify the omission. Thus, individual processes here were driven by organizational needs.

We see a similar discussion of individual and organizational processes in a discussion of sampling techniques from an engineering study protocol:

Writer: Basically here I am trying to—basically I'm trying to get those down on paper as to exactly what he [colleague] requires to make hard data . . . and then I was going to another paragraph to talk about the QA/QC samples, the additional samples that are required to get—to make sure that the samples have validity.

Reviewer: So you are talking about blind samples, and spike samples . . . My initial reaction is this . . . when you use the term "matrix spike" and what else . . .

Writer: "Matrix Spike Duplicate" and then sample delivery.

Reviewer: "two trip blanks"—uhm that probably should be explained because this protocol is something that a technical person might not be doing—it might be something that an individual might be doing. I think that either of these that you are using is going to be fine as long as you take the time to explain them. Was there any definition of matrix spike? Or you need to be QA/QC for each SDG? (Engineering, Simon, Textual Replay).

This engineer had personal motivations for choosing sampling techniques and explaining them: to satisfy requirements that surfaced in his previous conversation with a colleague as well as his own desire to "get those down on paper as to exactly what he requires to make hard data." The engineer started to make connections between his individual processes and other organizational processes. The reviewer extended this connection, noting that either of the samples would be fine "as long as [he took] time to explain them." The reviewer pointed to the fact that a field tech might be conducting the tests and might not be completely familiar with the engineer's accurate yet "kind of bizarre" explanation of the required samples. Finally, the reviewer tied the engineer's writing to QA/QC (quality assurance/quality control) issues to reinforce a point he made previously about the need for the samples to be robust enough for the lab.

The second type of rhetorical activity that the reviewers connected to composing practices concerned broader organizational activities in which the texts served as fixed kinds of mediation. Most of these rhetorical contextualizations happened at the Engineering Agency, for example:

> **Writer:** Then I was thinking, you know, like I really want to separate out these items—these emissions sources. . . . And so I wanted to keep each emissions source separate, and then what I end up doing is I go back and start making little paragraphs describing each of the emission sources.
> **Reviewer:** Right, because in a permit review report the emission unit description will comment on all of that; however, which way do you want to take it? The process is—it will ask you separately for process descriptions and those will be separated out automatically (Engineering, Duncan, Textual Replay).

The engineer's discussion of his motivations for writing (i.e., "I really want to separate out these items—these emissions sources") resulted in a convenient point of connection for the reviewer to talk about organizational processes that happened to match the engineer's motivations (i.e., "Right, because in a permit review report the emission unit description will comment on all of that"). The reviewer used his organizational knowledge that the permit-review reports require emissions sources to be listed separately to confirm that the engineer's writing strategy was effective.

For some of the rhetorical connections, the reviewed text was linked to a handful of other texts that were written by other members of the organization, all of which were intended to serve interrelated purposes. From the same review as the last example, the reviewer sketched out a larger textual context that ought to have shaped the engineer's intentions.

> **Reviewer:** Now are you just changing this in the permit review report? Or is this stuff that you put into the application itself?
> **Writer:** No, it was just the permit review report.
> **Reviewer:** So the permit review report still contains that information, the descriptions that the ...
> **Writer:** The application still has the application descriptions.
> **Reviewer:** Right.
> **Writer:** The little end caps and a really short, not very good description.
> **Reviewer:** But, and just the content too, right? I mean it doesn't include your extra additional descriptions, right?
> **Writer:** No.

Reviewer: Well, one suggestion is that the code is going to display whatever is in the application.

Writer: And not what is in the permit review report?

Reviewer: No, not what is in the permit review report. And that is okay, but if you know you have done a more complete job in the permit review report you might want the permit issued to show those more complete descriptions as well.

Writer: Oh, I see.

Reviewer: so you might want to change that to put it in the application so that it displays it in the permit as well (Engineering, Duncan, Textual Replay).

Looking at the writer's expanded descriptions of the emissions sources, the reviewer's first thought appeared to be about the other texts that connected to this one and the differences in how much description they required and provided. By asking the writer questions about the text and its place in relationship to the other texts, the reviewer created a richer picture of how different texts in the permit application process are connected. He also made a specific statement about the effects of providing such a rich level of detail, essentially that the permit application would need to contain the same rich level of description.

An explanation for the increase in rhetorical coordination is that the thread of organizational context was strong already. Organizational need was a primary concern in text-mediated writing reviews, and because the writers were already comfortable talking about such issues, there was enough organizational overlap to make coordination possible. At the same time, the rhetorical information appeared to become more meaningful because the presence of the textual replay enabled the writers and reviewers to draw in writing process to that discussion.

Despite the apparent utility of the textual replay in writing review at all organizations, the textual replay is not yet a complete technological answer. The actions of the writers and reviewers also revealed ways that the textual replay constrained writing review, by making it longer, and by introducing a new kind of cognitive effort (switching between editable and non-editable representations of text) both of which suggest improvements to make the textual replay a better tool. Revisions to the design of the textual replay and general comments about the role that scholars of professional and technical writing can play in technology development are the subjects of the final chapter.

CHAPTER 8

Designing Technology to Support Practice

This book has been about writing review, a topic that has been handled, ably, by many colleagues who have preceded me. One conclusion that we can make from the literature is that good writing review is built on supportive social interactions between writers and their reviewers. Where this study differs from my colleagues' is in its consideration of the technological environment in which the goals of effective writing review are pursued and social interactions between writers and reviewers are supported. This research takes the position that social interaction cannot be separated from the technology-rich environments in which they occur. In fact, social interaction is mediated by those technologies, whose increasing abundance and indispensability make it all the more important to investigate their connection to practices like writing review. Technologies like word processors, electronic libraries, e-mails, PDAs, content managements systems, and numerous others alter the shape and functionality of information and texts around which many work, professional, civic, and social practices are structured. These technologies help us perceive information as fixed or negotiable. They help us see texts as freestanding or connected. They help information appear official or unofficial. All of these factors then mediate our awareness of how information can be used and in service of what activities.

The impact of technology on writing review is no different. Writing review is an important part of enculturation (see Paradis, Dobrin, and Miller, 1985). It is an important site of experiential learning and mentoring (see Beaufort, 2000), and the goal is still to help writers find ways of being recognized as literate practitioners (Katz, 1998; MacKinnon, 1993). Technology does alter the scale, scope, and importance of this work. To some degree, information technology is an engine of complexity, producing texts as the byproducts of our interactions. The texts, also, become part of a distributed, cognitive architecture (see Devitt,

1991; Engeström and Middleton, 1998; Hutchins, 1995; Sellen and Harper, 2001) making it doubly important to produce good writing while at the same time making it more difficult to understand how.

Writing review that results in both enculturation and individuation requires a cooperative and pedagogical relationship between writers and reviewers. This kind of relationship is facilitated or constrained, in part, by the technological environments through which the writers and reviewers gain access to text and cooperate in its revision. While information technologies may be well designed to support obvious uses of text, they may not equally support less obvious uses like learning and teaching. A related factor is the social environment and the formal training that writers and reviewers bring with them.

Writers and reviewers at *Metronews* enter the writing review with the idea that the writing process is not finished. They come together to achieve a common understanding of what the text should do and to devise a course of action for moving the text in that direction. This kind of review is supported by technologies that support cooperative and distributed input on a single text. This technological mediation, the writers' and reviewers' shared training as professional writers, and *Metronews'* organizational environment created a review environment in which the writers both learned what it took to write an effective news story (enculturation) and identified opportunities to push their work in new directions (individuation).

In the absence of specific training and a favorable organizational environment, the positives and negatives of supporting technologies are amplified. In an organization like the Engineering Agency, where the goals for review are ostensibly the same, the technologies that adequately support everyday use of text also make review more challenging, because they portray texts as fixed information artifacts and because they hide evidence of the composing processes and motivations that brought them about. Information technologies at the Engineering Agency were set up to support interaction with texts that are stable, fixed, and reliably crafted for accountability and legal reasons, among others. The detrimental effect of technology is more pronounced in organizations like this because the reviewers and writers, alike, lack sufficient training to talk about writing process and sufficient motivation to understand why it is important. More of the burden falls on the supporting technologies, which must be designed to provide appropriate support.

Certainly writing review must be structured by organizational factors, but to fulfill its pedagogical aims, writing review requires its own technologically-mediated space. This space should be designed to support uses of text that writing professionals are uniquely qualified to investigate. This book has been an example of a methodology that we can apply toward the study of writing-related activities and to the technologies that support them. The remainder of the chapter is a design agenda for producing a textual replay technology that adequately supports various practices of writing review in different organizations. The goal is to show how design can follow from critical observations that writing and communication specialists are trained to make.

THE TECHNOLOGY OF TEXTUAL REPLAY

Textual replay does not exist, at least not yet. While I have used the term "textual replay" to describe the videos that writers and reviewers used to mediate their review practices, I have only done so as shorthand. Textual replay is an idea for a technology that would provide useful mediation for writing review by allowing presentation of the text as a particle and a stream of writing activity.

The technological intervention studied in these pages was by some measures successful and by other measures unsuccessful. And this result is to be expected. The challenge is to use the results of this study to make improvements. We should begin by recounting the kind of mediation that we would want from textual replay.

At the start of this project, I speculated that writing reviews taking place in artifact-oriented organizations would be hampered by two related problems. First, neither the writers nor the reviewers saw themselves as writers, nor did they see their principle professional work to be writing. As a result, they lacked a motivation for paying attention to issues related to writing process. They would also lack a common language for talking about process. Textual replay would first need to raise writing practice to a more prominent place in the review.

The second problem concerned the technological environments in which writing reviews took place. These environments reinforced a hard separation between the text as an organizational artifact and as a product of a writer's literate attempts to participate in streams of organizational activity. Composing was privatized by technologies like word processing programs and paper texts, which left evidence of process behind on the writers' computers and in their waste cans. Without a concrete representation of writing process, conversations about how writing process intersects with organizational interests would infrequently arise. Textual replay was intended to provide this information.

When faced with these problems, one cannot envision a perfect tool, but rather must start with a concept of the right kind of mediation that could promote the kinds of interactions that appeared to be missing. One starts by looking at other technologies that provide similar kinds of mediation in other settings.

The first precursor technology behind the textual replay was the instant replay and supporting point-of-view technologies. In sports like orienteering, head-mounted cameras are sometimes used to capture the athlete's view of the terrain. Microphones are used to capture the athlete's vocalized decision making (Omodei et al., 1998). After the fact, the coach and athlete can replay the tape and annotate it with information about the decision-making process, coordinating that information with real-time visual information about the performance itself. These perspectives combine in the replay medium, helping fuse advice about optimal performance with the recalled sensation of enacting those decisions.

The second precursor technology was screen capture technology that is often used in computer training. A screen capture records details of performance that a person might later overlook or forget. The screen capture makes a tangible record out of an ephemeral activity and elevates it to public view, where it can be scrutinized and accounted for in an after-the-fact explanation of performance.

The idea behind the textual replay is that writing is a performance that occurs in an environment where opportunities for over-the-shoulder instruction are constrained. Given that writing relies heavily on experiential knowledge, writing review would be better if it did allow over-the-shoulder perspectives on the writing process. For this reason, a point-of-view technology that records writing process seemed useful. Further, because writing reviews at artifact-oriented organizations took place between people who felt some professional distance from issues of writing, a technology that created a tangible representation of it might make conversations about process more likely. Another concern was that for writers to learn how to produce good writing, the reviewers needed to talk more about writing process and to look past the static, fixed form of text with which they most typically dealt. For this reason, the technology would need to support a "stream" view of text as opposed to a "particle" view only.

The textual replay provided approximations of these kinds of mediation—to some positive effects. In the practice-oriented and artifact-oriented organizations alike, there was more talk about writing process. The revision suggestions were more facilitative. The writers participated more. The reviewers worked with writers on revisions. To be expected, however, there were also problems. The first set of problems might be best described as text-handling problems, operational issues that made use of the textual replays cumbersome. Writers needed to manipulate the screen capture technology manually. Transport of the massive video files was troublesome, even across company intranets. Finding compatible media players and downloading the appropriate compression and decompression codecs was problematic. Further, common media players were designed to handle music and video files, not necessarily 12-point Times New Roman, which was frequently unreadable without making adjustments to the viewer. These operational problems may explain why the textual replay-mediated reviews averaged about 2:07 minutes longer than text-mediated reviews (nearly a 10% increase).

In addition to physical difficulties, the textual replays also introduced additional cognitive burdens. While textual replay did effectively disrupt the "particle" view of text that was rigidly portrayed on paper, it moved too far in the other direction, locking viewers into a "stream" perspective. The problem was that writers and reviewers frequently needed to switch between "particle" and "stream" views. Often, the participants talked about writing process as it pertained to a particular section of text. Once the reviewers understood what happened, they looked at the text in order to revise it.

The second type of problem concerned the ways in which writers and reviewers could interact with the text shown in the textual replay. When the writers and reviewers looked at the text developing over time, they occasionally saw iterations of sentences, paragraphs, and sections that they wanted to keep, an activity that the textual reply significantly constrained. While the textual replay made it possible to see the different particles in a stream of writing activity, it did not make it easy to separate the particles from one another.

To sum up the most pressing problem: the textual replay is not an editable medium. The review participants may pause the replay to show the text at a given moment in time, but that version cannot be captured and edited. As a result, the writers and reviewers did not relieve themselves of the need to coordinate talk about process with actual revisions. In fact, the textual replay created another kind of coordination problem, bringing together past versions of a text with the version currently captured on paper.

A related problem is that the textual replay only made the writer's experiential knowledge more accessible. It did not provide much insight into the experiences that the reviewers brought to bear on the text. In the case of practice-oriented organizations, the textual replay appeared to provide a comprehensive account of experiences that the writers and reviewers both thought meaningful. Only when the textual replay was applied to writing reviews in artifact-oriented organizations did it become clear that another kind of relevant experience was without concrete representation: the reviewer's experience of the mediating functions that texts served throughout an organization. This knowledge derived from how the reviewers experienced texts and their utility in the context of specific work practices. Many of the texts that the engineers wrote, for instance, had strong ties to other texts. In the reviews are glimpses of those connections, but no tangible, shareable record that could help the writers make those same connections and link them to their experience of composing.

Text-Handling Changes

The first category of changes must deal with the ways that the writers and reviewers access and use texts. Part of the advantage of textual replay is that it was different from paper. Yet the extent of the difference also proved problematic, as there are mediating qualities of paper that are worth retaining. The textual replay asked the writer and reviewers to compromise on many of the key affordances that Sellen and Harper (2001, pp. 101-103) attribute to paper, among which are "spatial flexibility"—the ability to easily move paper around (p. 102), and "manipulability"—the ability to put texts together and switch attention between them (p. 103). These qualities are integral to the conduct of writing review, yet constrained by the textual replay.

Among the most problematic aspects of the textual replay was its lack of "spatial flexibility." The screen capture program used to create the textual replays outputted .avi video files that, even for very short writing sessions, produced very large files, often several megabytes. As a result, the files were difficult to move. Even after successfully transferring them between computers, using them required appropriate software, drivers, and codecs. Further, the textual reply required the participants to conduct the review at a computer. All of these factors added up to a mediating technology that was not very spatially flexible.

Some of the problems mentioned above will improve as screen capture technology does. Files sizes will go down, the compression and decompression codecs will become more common. However, there are some design improvements that could be enacted to enhance the portability of the outputted files and increase the likelihood that they will be used. The place to start is to help the textual replay become more selective about what it records during the composing process.

One aspect of the textual replay that frustrated reviewers and writers alike was that the software captured moments of writing activity and inactivity. The textual replays captured long, ponderous gaps in onscreen writing activity as the writers re-read what they had written, thought about what to write, answered the phone, or talked with a colleague. On the playback, one cannot tell what the pause represents, and it only adds bulk to the file. Instead of asking the writers to start and stop the program (which could lead to impression management), the textual replay could be linked to the word-processing software by attaching a shutter release command to a keyboard function (e.g., pressing the space bar) so that the screen is recorded continuously only while content is being generated. This improvement would keep the file size to a minimum while maximizing the information that it holds.

Another problem is related to the affordance of "manipulability." One can fold paper, tear it, and hold it next to other sheets of paper, but the textual replay was far more constrained. Where writers and reviewers would put multiple texts together in text-mediated reviews and then switch attention between them, such coordination of attention was more difficult with the textual replay. Not only did the participants need to shift attention between the computer and the paper, but also between a "stream" and a "particle" view, which required different ways of thinking about the text.

Another affordance of paper that is related to manipulability is that it is possible to access the text non-linearly. Headings and paragraphs, for instance, make it possible for the readers to see the text as comprised of modular units of information. The screen capture program did not offer similar access, meaning that it would take some time for the participants to find the section of the video that they wished to show. The extra scrolling, searching, and scanning certainly must have accounted for some of the increased time for the textual-replay-mediated writing reviews. The textual replay literally captured writing activity, but could not separate moments in that process. The outputted video file contained no marks or breaks that would indicate start and stop points. The only start and stop points were those that the writers added with the screen capture's production manager.

To be useful in a writing review, the textual replays ought to allow more flexible access. Access could be improved by chunking the video into smaller parts, which correspond to contiguous writing activities. The chunking could be achieved automatically by piggybacking a cutting function to a keyboard command, like the enter key. For example, whenever the writer would hit the enter key, the textual replay program would splice together the frames taken since the last enter keystroke, and save the version as a separate video file. Any subsequent revisions to that paragraph would then save out as threaded video segments, differentiated from one another by the time of their creation and their placement in the text. When the review participants would come to a section of text that they wanted to see animated, they could select the textual replay from a context menu.

By making changes to the text handling features of the textual replay, we will also end up changing the ways that the textual replay supports writer and reviewer interaction and their interaction with the text. Within practice-oriented and artifact-oriented organizations alike, there are beneficial writer/review interactions that one would want to keep and which can be enhanced by making some changes to the textual replay interface.

Interactivity Changes

Another consequence of the move to textual replay is that it alters the "tangibility" or the basic materiality (Sellen and Harper, 2001, p. 101) of the text, as well as its "tailorability"—paper's capacity for accepting marks and annotations (p. 102; see also Swarts, 2004b). First, consider the impact on tangibility. Many information technologies have an impact on the tangibility of the information that they hold. Technologies like electronic libraries make texts tangible as clusters of related texts. Word processing software makes texts tangible at the level of words and page design. Some page design tools make text tangible at a more granular level still, allowing writers to alter the look and feel of the letters themselves. These differences in tangibility correspond to different kinds of tasks, each of which require texts to be fixed or fluid at different levels. Print has the same effect.

With printed text, one loses access to the words on the page and to the page-level design elements. The artifact is presented not as a collection of sentences and paragraphs, but as a text. Paper helps fix information and perhaps discourages changes, working against the purpose of writing review. As we have seen, presentation of a draft on paper may contribute to reviews that focus on a text's artifactual qualities more so than on the writing decisions on which it is built. This is not to say that paper has no place in writing review, but rather that we should learn to recognize its complementary value next to textual replay. As we saw in Chapters 6 and 7, as the writers and reviewers started to interact as writers, they increasingly used the paper both to ground their perceptions of the text's artifactual responsibilities and to hold representations of the changes that they recommended. Paper was important to coordination and cooperation.

Even as the writers and reviewers used the textual replay, they returned their attention to the paper text to make revision suggestions. As noted in the last section, the need to switch attention between the mediating technologies introduced a new kind of coordination burden to link talk about writing process to organizational contexts and from that to actual revision suggestions. One of the root problems was that the textual replay did not make the text tangible at all of the necessary levels. By comparison, text was the more suitable medium. To avoid the problems associated with sustaining coordination, we ought to change the levels at which the textual replay allows tangible access to the text.

At times during review, the writers and reviewers interacted best by talking about the text as a stream of writing activity. At other times, they wanted to move in closer to a particle view, in which they could interact with the text as a set of word and design choices. Complicating this picture, some reviewers wanted to work with iterations of the text that no longer existed except as frames on the textual replay. That is, some reviewers pointed to wording, organization, and development that was not present in the paper text, but was visible in the textual replay. This conflict underscores one of the key reasons why textual replay can be valuable. The paper text is a particulate representation of a writing process, but it is only *one* view, and it is only the *latest* view. What happens when writers and reviewers want to extract text from some point in the past? The textual replay does not provide that level of access.

The current form of textual replay also hinders revision, a key component of the review process. In the textual replay tested here, the participants needed to leave the textual replay and return to the text in order to make revisions. These changes, though, were removed from the artifact that represented the "writing process," a move that appeared to impede what Schön (1987) called "reflection in action" (pp. 26-27). We may achieve this fusion of product and process by making textual replay a medium that supports revision. Ideally, the review participants could stop a textual replay, select a moment in that text's history, produce a transfer copy, and make revisions based on the draft as it existed. To conceive of how such edits would be possible, we might think about tracing paper, where the reviewer could lay a piece of tracing paper over any frame in the textual replay, peel it away, and take it to a word processing program.

Tangibility also must move in the other direction, making the writer's text more concrete as an intertextually-bound organizational artifact. Katz (1998b) suggested that one of the more important steps a reviewer should take in socializing a new writer is to "contextualize the task." That is, the "information or procedure must be presented within the context of a typical situation" (p. 168), and we know that one aspect of the writing context is the ecology of texts, people, and resources to which the text is connected. To make textual replay a tool that supports cooperative framing and discussion of the text, the tool needs to make available textual qualities that are consistent with the reviewers' experience as writers.

The textual replay was conceived of as a way to present text as a stream of writing activity. The argument was that without that information, reviewers from artifact-oriented organizations would be more inclined to evaluate the texts as organizational artifacts instead of equally as acts of writing practice. These reviewers understand how texts connect to one another, how information migrates between texts, but may be less aware of and concerned with the more local context of writing and revision that a draft text still needs to mediate.

To some extent, these speculations turned out wrong. The reviewers at the artifact-oriented organizations did appear more concerned with rhetorical and organizational issues, but they were not as effective at talking about them as anticipated. The textual replay did help eliminate some of the distance between organizational realities and the writer's composing experiences, but it did not create a rich enough particle view from which the reviewers could articulate what they knew about organizational circumstances. While the reviewers did get better at talking about writing process, an unintended, but still quite interesting side effect of talking about the text at that level was that the reviewers increased their discussion of rhetorical issues and more frequently connected those issues to a discussion of composing processes, motivations, and intentions. Yet this discussion remained fairly abstract.

A design requirement that might make the organizational context of a review text clearer would be to support an online reviewing environment in which we could see different views of the text, such as the process view that the textual replay currently provides, but also, perhaps, an organizational view that would include: a flow chart of organizational processes to which a text is a contribution; a hypertext map of related documents and resources that borrow language, data, and sources from the text under review; and a use-history map showing who has accessed the text. A design goal would be to let the organizational view be self-generating, a map of use that is built from a computer system's awareness of how a text has been accessed, updated, copied, and otherwise manipulated.

Another important affordance of text to retain is its tailorability. With paper, the writers and reviewers made many different marks. As I pointed out in some of the reviews at *Metronews*, the editor made written marks in order to record some version of a comment or revision. At Donor Relations, one of the reviewers frequently used paper copies of the solicitation letters to insert rhetorical information that helped ground the text as an organizational object (Swarts, 2004b). Tailorability is important to writing review because it allows the users to mark a text with information that assists in coordination-building.

The textual replay did not accept marks, although the writers and reviewers verbally marked them with information and meaning that was apparently intended to create common ground and to serve as a point of mediation for future revisions. The writers marked the textual replays with information about process. The reviewers marked them with information about rhetorical context. If the writers are to use the textual replays to mediate future writing activity, then we might envision some changes to allow useful annotations.

To make verbal annotations, the reviewer could open an audio channel during the review and lay in an audio track over the writing activity on the screen. Hypothetically, reviewers and writers could put in multiple audio layers. To make written annotations, the reviewers and writers may use a touch pen to insert comments directly on to the textual replay. The result of both kinds of annotations would be an artifact that is enhanced with process and contextual information that the writer could access in order to recall relevant points during the revision.

The Role of Writing Specialists

One question that remains concerns the role of writing and communication specialists. The issues of technology design would appear to be better suited to engineers and those in the computer sciences, but it is precisely because we have left questions of information design exclusively to these professionals that we see some of the problems that I have discussed. I am not suggesting that writing and communication specialists should replace these professionals. Instead, I am suggesting that we can work with them.

The context of the problem outlined in this book should alone help underscore the role that we can play influencing the development of information technology. Every year the base of information technology continues to develop and proliferate. People from many diverse professions interact with their technologies and turn their knowledge and observations into texts that they share with others and that they use to support the work of others in globally and socially distributed organizations. This is the age of Reich's "symbolic analyst" come to life, and the practical consequence is that many professionals, regardless of training, are becoming writers who are responsible for producing texts on which others depend.

The sheer number of texts aside, we must also pay attention to the technological architectures that have been built up for creating, storing, and sharing these texts. In many cases, they have unforeseen impacts on other text-mediated activities that may not be obvious to technology designers. Technologies change how information is represented to users and how the texts communicate their uses to those audiences. These are communication problems that would be well addressed by people who study such phenomena.

From the news that we read, to the air quality regulations that protect us, and to the ways that our lives have become instantiated in these text-centric systems, written communication is increasingly playing a vital mediating function in our lives. If we continue to proliferate technologies that create texts out of our everyday experiences and put texts at the center of our interactions with other people, then the input of specialists in our field is essential. Getting started only requires a willingness to look at technologies as agents in communicative practices and the confidence that we have something valuable to add to conversations about technology development. It is my sincere hope that this book has taken us a step in that direction.

Glossary

Artifact: any text described in terms of its objective mediational value to specific organizational processes and practices rather than to the private writing process that brought it about.

Artifact-Oriented: describing organizations where writers do not consider themselves to be professional writers, and where reviewers focus their attention on texts as organizational artifacts (see Artifact).

Artifactual Architecture: an arrangement of technologies, resources, conventions of practice, and people that reinforce an *artifact-oriented* approach to writing review (see Artifact, Artifact-Oriented, Practice Architecture, Practice-Oriented).

Cognitive Architecture: a network of *artifacts* on to which people offload cognitive effort for interpretation, calculation, information sharing, transformation, and all manner of cognitive and information processing tasks.

Coordination: instances of conversation during a writing review when writer and reviewer both talk about a text in terms of the same qualities: Text, Process, Rhetorical, Content (see Coordination-building Device).

Coordination-building Device: linguistic objects such as questions, proposals, corrections, and suggestions that encourage a response from an interlocutor (see Coordination).

Enculturation: a process by which a newcomer develops the ability to both contribute to organizational *practices*, *processes*, and culture while also recognizing ways to change them (see Individuation).

Fixed: in texts, a quality referring to the degree that information appears rigid and unchanging (see Fluid).

Fluid: in texts, a quality referring to the degree that information appears to be in flux and changing (see Fixed).

Horizontal Coordination: coordination of work *practices* among those people performing complementary tasks in an organization (see Vertical Coordination).

Individuation: the process by which a newcomer learns to actively change organizational culture and assert him/herself as an integral part of the organization (see Enculturation).

Mediate/Mediation: a process by which the application of a tool to a task helps structure and clarify the task in ways that are not inherent to the task itself (see Meta-Mediation).

Meta-Mediation: a multiplied effect of mediation wherein two or more mediating artifacts are layered together to provide sufficiently rich task mediation (see Mediation).

Particle (View): a technologically-supported view of text in which the words, sentences, and paragraphs on the page appear static and finished (see Mediation, Stream (View)).

Practice: localized, messy, ad hoc work activities through which the work of an organization is carried out (see Process).

Practice Architecture: an arrangement of technologies, resources, conventions of practice, and people that reinforce a *practice-oriented* approach to writing review (see Artifact, Artifact-Oriented, Practice-Oriented).

Practice-Oriented: describing organizations where writers do consider themselves to be professional writers and where reviewers focus their attention equally on the work that a text does as an organizational artifact and as the product of a writing process (see Artifact-Oriented).

Process: a formalized description of observed regularities in organizational work practices (see Practice).

Review Architecture: an arrangement of technologies, resources, conventions of practice, and people that support writing review (see Artifact Architecture, Practice Architecture).

Reviewers: those people in an organization (usually supervisors or more experienced peers) charged with reading, marking, and approving texts before they are widely circulated.

Stream (View): a technologically-supported view of text in which the words, sentences, and paragraphs on the page appear as actions or dramatizations of writing practice (see Mediation, Particle (View)).

Vertical Coordination: coordination of work *practices* among those people performing the same tasks in an organization (see Horizontal Coordination).

Writing Review: a practice in which a writer submits a draft of his/her text to a *reviewer*, who reads, evaluates, and discusses options or requirements for revising it.

Appendix A

This appendix contains a summary of the differences between Text-Mediated and Textual-Replay-Mediated Writing Reviews.

Dyads	Text Mediation			Textual Replay Mediation			
	Date	Length	Text	Date	Length	Text	Times TR used
Metronews							
Tina with Randall	6/20/01	20:36	Newstory	6/12/01	21:33	Newstory	47
Diane with Randall	5/24/01	14:00	Newstory	6/7/01	17:15	Newstory	120
Celia with Randall	8/17/01	22:34	Newstory	7/19/01	22:01	Newstory	101
Media Relations I							
Jessica with Bailey	4/17/01	14:48	Press release	6/01/01	15:00	Press release	29
Petra with Bailey	11/1/01	10:27	Press release	10/24/01	20:07	Press release	64
Media Relations II							
Ben with Susan	9/25/01	17:03	Press release	10/24/01	17:45	Press release	54
Donor Relations							
Charles with Mary	8/3/01	46:41	Letter	7/19/01	28:40	Letter	226
Linda with Mary	7/9/01	45:33	Spending proposal	8/13/01	27:21	Spending proposal	165
Ivan with Deb	6/29/01	18:05	Contract	7/16/01	32:33	Review	148
Engineering Agency							
Bill with Rick	9/30/01	10:50	Regulations	10/18/01	13:54	Regulations	55
Duncan with Earl	9/14/01	11:56	Permit Review	8/29/01	38:13	Schedule of Compliance	233
Simon with Eric	8/29/01	15:49	Protocol	9/19/01	15:22	Protocol	52

Appendix B

This appendix contains the complete coding definitions that were applied to the segmented transcripts of the writing review sessions.

Text

Code as "text" all direct or clarified pronominal (i.e., it [first sentence]) references to the text and its appearance. Do not code references to the "meaning" of the text. Include:

- references to different versions of the text (e.g., "is this on my copy?" "we are on paper, now")
- references to the actual or proposed wording of the text (e.g., "this needs to read (the meeting will be at 7:00)")
- references to sections of text designated by their content (e.g., "end with 'the judge ordered that'")
- references to parts of a text (e.g., "sentence," "text," "paragraph," "word"—for example "look at this paragraph")
- references to formatting (e.g., "put that in bold," "bullet this")
- references to generic locations in the text (e.g., "top," "middle," "end")
- references to the entire document (e.g., "this press release is good")

Rhetorical

Code as "rhetorical" all direct or clarified pronominal (i.e., it [first sentence]) references to the rhetorical context or effect of a text. Include:

- evaluations of the text (e.g., "I think your descriptions are good," "this section is overwhelming," "The text seems so everyday.")

- references to the audience and/or their expectations (e.g., "they already know this"),
- references to the purpose of the text and/or its expected outcomes (e.g., "the lab needs a method that they can rely on to make hard data")
- references to the writer's external exigence (e.g., "deadline," "receipt of a gift," "lawsuit") or internal motivations (e.g., "I wanted to bring this out") for writing.
- references to people or institutions
- references to structuring or arrangement devices (e.g., outlines, sketches, notes, etc.)
- references to the genre or its features (e.g., "essentially this a compliance schedule," "I think that you might use a feature/lede")
- references to abstract "rules" of writing (e.g., "I thought that the lede should stand on its own," "according to stone cold journalism, this breaks a lot of rules")
- references to texts other than the text under review (e.g., "refer to the 82-3?")
- references to the function of sections in the text (e.g., "this is for comparison")

Content

Code as "content" any direct or clarified pronominal (i.e., it [first sentence]) references to the meaning of the text. Content references establish "what" was said and not "how" it was said. Include:

- references to the "gist" of a text or individual statement (e.g., "the piece is to tell people about the **** Fellowship.")
- instances when the reviewer or reader is "reader aloud" (always indicated by "double quotes")
- references to correct grammar, spelling, tense, and syntax (e.g., "I'm not sure why this is a declarative," "you have the tense wrong," "this is what the grammarians would call unparallel")
- discussion of the ideas in a text (e.g., "we don't know that there is a problem, but we suspect that there is," "what do you mean by 'institutional?'")
- discussion of background material (information related to the meaning of the text but not directly to the composition of it (e.g., "I interviewed him on Thursday" where "him" refers to the person the story is about)

Process

Code as "process" any direct or clarified pronominal (i.e., it [first sentence]) references to composing activity. Include:

- references to planned but (as yet) incomplete revisions (e.g., "I am going to move this paragraph to the top")

- references to revisions already completed (indicated by past tense verbs) (e.g., "I eventually made that 2 sentences")

- references to composing activity visible on the textual replay (always indicated by ((double parentheses))—even if in "future tense" (e.g., ((so now you are cleaning up your wording?)), ((you will see that I get rid of that paragraph))

- references to a writer's process (e.g., "you made this draft and then took it to xxxx," "run this past xxxx")

- references to action verbs that indicate composing activity (always code the following no matter the tense: "say," "made," "do," "put in," "inserted")

- references to strategies—demonstrated or recommended (e.g., "you highlighted these points," "stay consistent," "can we bring out [university] participation?")

Directive

Second
Pass

Code as directive, any t-unit wherein the writer or reviewer makes a revision suggestion and coordination is assumed or the writer's participation is not invited. *A revision suggestion is only an instance where the reviewer asks or tells the writer to do something to the text.*

Include:

- Commands—the reviewer or writer tells the other person to "do" or "say" something (e.g., "say . . ." "do it this way").

- Revision suggestions using obligatory modals (always code suggestions using "ought," "shall," "should," "need to," "must," "will," "would").

- Evaluations—where the reviewer or the writer evaluates the text (e.g., "this is good," "this is not working," "you are not achieving what you want")

- Corrections—when the reviewer physically rewrites the text (such instances are always indicated by [[double square brackets]].

Facilitative

Code as facilitative, any t-unit wherein the writer or reviewer makes a revision suggestion or asks a question where the speaker invites participation by the writer. *A revision suggestion is only an instance where the reviewer asks or tells the writer to do something to the text.*

Include:

- Proposals—where the reviewer or the writer suggests a course of revision, intending it to be a suggestion. Often introduced with question words ("who," "what," "where," "when," "why")

- Questions—designated as [question]. When they appear at the end of a revision suggestion, they should always be coded as facilitative.

- Conditional modals—always code as facilitative ("may," "might," "can," "could," "perhaps," "maybe," "if," "unless," and "I think"). Also include use of the word "probably" when not accompanied by any obligatory modals (see Directive).

- Alternatives—if the reviewer offers a different way to revise ("you could do . . . or you could . . .") nearly every use of "or" will be facilitative.

References

Bakhtin, M. M. (1986). *Speech genres and other late essays.* C. Emerson and M. Holquist (Eds.). Austin, TX: University of Texas Press.

Bateson, G. (1972). *Steps to an ecology of mind.* New York: Ballantine.

Bazerman, C. (1994). Systems of genres and the enactment of social intentions. In A. Freedman and P. Medway (Eds.), *Genres and the new rhetoric* (pp. 79-101). London: Taylor and Francis.

Bazerman, C. (2000a). Singular utterances: Realizing local activities through typified forms in typified circumstances. In A. Trosborg (Ed.), *Analyzing professional genres* (pp. 25-40). Philadelphia: John Benjamins Publishing.

Bazerman, C. (2000b). *Textual performance: Where the action at a distance is.* Paper presented at Rhetoric Society of America Conference. Washington, DC.

Bazerman, C. (2003a). What is not institutionally visible does not count: The problem of making activity assessable, accountable, and plannable. In C. Bazerman and D. Russell (Eds.), *Writing selves/Writing societies: Research from activity perspectives.* Retrieved December 5, 2005 from http://wac.colostate.edu/books/writing_selves/.

Bazerman, C. (2003b). Speech acts, genres, and activity Systems: How texts organize activity and people. In C. Bazerman and P. Prior (Eds.), *What writing does and how it does it: An introduction to analyzing texts and textual practices* (pp. 309-340). Mahwah, NJ: Lawrence Erlbaum Associates.

Bazerman, C., Little, J., and Chavkin, T. (2003). The production of information for genred activity spaces: Informational motives and consequences of the environmental impact statement. *Written Communication, 20*(4), 455-477.

Beaufort, A. (2000). Learning the trade: A social apprenticeship model for gaining writing expertise. *Written Communication, 17,* 185-223.

Berkenkotter, C., and Huckin, T. N. (1994). *Genre knowledge in disciplinary communication: Cognition/culture/power.* Hillsdale, NJ: Lawrence Erlbaum Associates.

Bernhardt, S. A. (2003). Improving document review practices in pharmaceutical companies. *Journal of Business and Technical Communication, 17*(4), 439-473.

Bolter, J. D. (2001). *Writing space: Computers, Hypertext, and the remediation of print* (2nd ed.). Mahwah, NJ: Lawrence Erlbaum.

Brown, J. S., and Duguid, P. (2000). *The social life of information.* Cambridge, MA: Harvard Business School Press.

Brun-Cottan, F., and Wall, P. (1995). Using video to re-present the user. *Communications of the ACM, 38*(5), 61-71.

Carley, K., and Kaufer, D. (1993). Semantic connectivity: An approach for analyzing symbols in semantic networks. *Communication Theory, 3*(3), 183-213.

Carley, K., and Palmquist, M. (1992). Extracting, representing, and analyzing mental models . *Social Force, 70*(3), 601-636.

Churchill, E. F., and Munro, A. J. (2001). WORK/PLACE: Mobile technologies and arenas of activity. *SIGGRROUP Bulletin, 22*(3), 3-9.

Clark, H. H. (1996). *Using language.* New York: Cambridge University Press.

Cohn, E., and Kleimann, S. (1989). *Writing to please your boss.* Rockville, MD: Scandinavian PC Press.

Cushman, E. (1998). *The struggle and the tools: Oral and literate strategies in an inner city community.* Albany, NY: State University of New York Press.

Devitt, A. J. (1991). Intertextuality in tax accounting: Generic, referential and functional. In C. Bazerman and J. Paradis (Eds.), *Textual dynamics of the professions: Historical and contemporary studies of writing in professional communities* (pp. 336-357). Madison, WI: University of Wisconsin Press.

Doheny-Farina, S. (1986). Writing in an emerging organization: An ethnographic study. *Written Communication, 3*(2), 158-185.

Douglas, M. (1986). *How institutions think.* Syracuse, NY: Syracuse University Press.

Flower, L., and Hayes, J. R. (1981). A cognitive process theory of writing. *College Composition and Communication, 32*(4), 365-387.

Gee, J., Hull, G., and Lankshear, C. (1996). *New work order.* Boulder, CO: Westview Press.

Geisler, C. (1994). *Academic literacy and the nature of expertise: Reading, writing, and knowing in academic philosophy.* Hillsdale, NJ: Lawrence Erlbaum Associates.

Geisler, C. (2001). Textual objects: Accounting for the role of texts in the everyday life of complex organizations. *Written Communication, 18,* 296-325.

Geisler, C. (2004). *Analyzing streams of language: Twelve steps to the systematic coding of text, talk, and other verbal data.* New York: Pearson Longman.

Gillette, D. (2001). Metaphorical confusion and spatial mapping in an age of ubiquitous computing. *Technical Communication, 48*(1), 42-48.

Goodwin, C., and Goodwin, M. (1998). Seeing as situated activity: Formulating planes. In Y. Engeström and D. Middleton (Eds.), *Cognition and communication at work* (pp. 61-95). New York: Cambridge University Press.

Goody, J. (1987). *The interface between the written and the oral.* New York: Cambridge University Press.

Goody, J., and Watt, I. (1968). The consequences of literacy. In J. Goody (Ed.), *Literacy in traditional societies,* Cambridge: Cambridge University Press.

Heath, C., and Luff, P. (1998). Convergent activities: Line control and passenger information on the London Underground. In Y. Engeström and D. Middleton (Eds.), *Cognition and communication at work* (pp. 96-129). New York: Cambridge University Press.

Heath, S. B. (1983). *Ways with words: Language, life, and work in communities and classrooms.* New York: Cambridge University Press.

Henderson, K. (1991). Flexible sketches and inflexible databases: Visual communication, conscription devices, and boundary objects in design engineering. *Science, Technology, and Human Values, 16*(4), 448-473.

Henderson, K. (1998). *Online and on paper: Visual representations, visual culture, and computer graphics in design engineering.* Cambridge, MA: Massachusetts Institute of Technology Press.

Henry, J. (2000). *Writing workplace cultures: An archaeology of professional writing.* Carbondale, IL: Southern Illinois University Press.

Herrington, A. (1983). *Writing in academic settings: A study of the rhetorical contexts for writing in two college chemical engineering courses.* Unpublished doctoral dissertation. Rensselaer Polytechnic Institute, Troy, NY.

Hollan, J., Hutchins, E., and Kirsh, D. (2000). Distributed cognition: Toward a new foundation for human-computer interaction research. *ACM Transactions on Computer-Human Interaction, 7,* 174-196.

Howard, V. (1984). *Artistry: The work of artists.* Indianapolis, IN: Hackett Press.

Hutchins, E. (1995). *Cognition in the wild.* Cambridge, MA: Massachusetts Institute of Technology Press.

Hutchins, E. (1997). Mediation and automatization. In Y. Engeström, and O. Vasquez (Eds.), *Mind, culture, and activity* (pp. 338-353). New York: Cambridge University Press.

Katz, S. M. (1998). *The dynamics of writing review.* Westport, CT: Ablex.

Katz, S. M. (1998a). Part I—Learning to writing in organizations: What newcomers learn about writing on the job. *IEEE Transactions on Professional Communication, 41*(2), 107-115.

Katz, S. M. (1998b). Part II—How newcomers learn to write: Resources for guiding newcomers. *IEEE Transactions on Professional Communication, 41*(3), 165-174.

Kleimann, S. M. (1993). The reciprocal nature of workplace culture and review. In R. Spilka (Ed.), *Writing in the workplace: New research perspectives* (pp. 21-40). Carbondale, IL: Southern Illinois University Press.

Kostelnick, C., and Roberts, D. D. (1998). *Designing visual language.* Boston, MA: Allyn and Bacon.

Latour, B. (1986). Visualization and cognition: Thinking with eyes and hands. *Knowledge and Society, 6,* 1-40.

Latour, B. (1995). Mixing humans and nonhumans together: The sociology of the door-closer. In S. L. Star (Ed.), *Ecologies of knowledge: Work and politics in science and technology* (pp. 257-277). Albany, NY: State University of New York Press.

Latour, B. (1996). On interobjectivity. Online. Available: http://www.ensmp.fr/~latour/articles/article/063.html.

Lave, J., and Wenger, L. (1991). *Situated learning: Legitimate peripheral practice.* New York: Cambridge University Press.

Levy, D. M. (1994). Fixed or fluid? Document stability and new media. *Proceedings of ECHT Conference,* pp. 24-31.

Levy, D. M. (2001). *Scrolling forward: Making sense of documents in the digital age.* New York: Arcade Press.

Luff, P., Heath, C., and Greatbatch, D. (1992). Tasks-in-interaction: Paper and screen based documentation in collaborative activity. *Proceedings of Computer Supported Cooperative Work*, pp. 163-170.

Lutz, J. A. (1989). Writers in organizations and how they learn the image: Theory, research, and implications. In C. B. Matalene (Ed.), *Worlds of Writing: Teaching and Learning in Discourse Communities of Work* (pp. 113-135). New York: Random House.

MacKinnon, J. (1993). Becoming a rhetor: Developing writing ability in a mature, writing-intensive organization. In R. Spilka (Ed.), *Writing in the workplace: New research perspectives* (pp. 41-55). Carbondale, IL: Southern Illinois University Press.

Mack, R., and Robinson, J. B. (1996). When novices elicit knowledge: Question asking in designing, evaluating, and learning to use software. In R. R. Hoffman (Ed.), *The Psychology of Expertise: Cognitive Research and Empirical AI* (pp. 245-268). New York: Springer-Verlag.

Matsuhashi, A. (1979). *Producing written discourse: A theory-based description of the temporal characteristics of three discourse types from four competent grade 12 writers.* Unpublished doctoral dissertation, Buffalo, NY.

Matsuhashi, A. (1981). Pausing and planning: The tempo of written discourse production. *Research in the Teaching of English, 15*(2), 113-134.

Medway, P. (1996). Virtual and material buildings: Construction and constructivism in architecture and writing. *Written Communication, 13,* 473-514.

Miller, C. R. (1984). Genre as social action. *Quarterly Journal of Speech, 70*(2), 151-167.

Mitchell, W. J. (1995). *City of bits: Space, place, and the infobahn.* Cambridge, MA: Massachusetts Institute of Technology Press.

Nardi, B. A., and O'Day, V. L. (1999). *Information ecologies: Using technology with heart.* Cambridge, MA: Massachusetts Institute of Technology Press.

Odell, L., Goswami, D., and Herrington, A. (1983). The discourse-based interview: A procedure for exploring tacit knowledge of writers in nonacademic settings. In P. Mosenthal, L. Tamor, and S. Wolmsley (Eds.), *Research on writing: Principles and methods* (pp. 220-236). New York: Longman.

Olson, D. R. (1996). *The world on paper: The conceptual and cognitive implications of writing and reading.* New York: Cambridge University Press.

Omodei, M. M., McLennan, J., and Whitford, P. (1998). Using a head-mounted video camera and two-stage replay to enhance orienteering performance. *International Journal of Sports Psychology, 29,* 115-131.

Paradis, J., Dobrin, D., and Miller, R. (1985). Writing at Exxon ITD: Notes on the writing environment of an R&D organization. In L. Odell and D. Goswami (Eds.), *Writing in Nonacademic Settings* (pp. 281-307). New York: Guilford Press.

Polanyi, M. (1962). *Personal knowledge: Towards a post-critical philosophy.* Chicago, IL: Chicago University Press.

Polanyi, M. (1974). *Personal knowledge: Towards a post-critical philosophy.* Chicago, IL: Chicago University Press.

Polanyi, M. (1983). *The tacit dimension.* New York: Peter Smith Publisher.

Prior, P. (1998). *Writing/Disciplinarity: A sociohistoric account of literate activity in the academy.* Mahwah, NJ: Lawrence Erlbaum Associates.

Reich, R. (1992). *The work of nations*. New York: Vintage.

Reich, R. (2003). Bringing back manufacturing. Online. Available: http://www.robertreich.org/reich/20030917.asp?view=print.

Ryle, G. (1949). *The concept of mind*. Chicago: University of Chicago Press.

Sauer, B. (1998). Embodied knowledge: The textual representation of embodied sensory information in a dynamic and uncertain material environment. *Written Communication, 15*(2), 131-169.

Schön, D. (1987). *Educating the reflective practitioner: Toward a new design for teaching and learning in the disciplines*. San Francisco, CA: Jossey-Bass.

Schriver, K. (1989). Evaluating text quality: The continuum from text-focused to reader-focused methods. *IEEE Transactions on Professional Communication, 32*, 238-255.

Schriver, K. (1997). *Dynamics in document design*. San Francisco, CA: Jossey Bass.

Schryer, C. F., and Spoel, P. (2005). Genre theory, health-care discourse, and professional identity formation. *Journal of Business and Technical Communication, 19*(3), 249-278.

Scribner, S., and Cole, M. (1981). *The psychology of literacy*. Cambridge, MA: Harvard University Press.

Sellen, A. J., and Harper, R. H. R. (2002). *The myth of the paperless office*. Cambridge, MA: Massachusetts Institute of Technology Press.

Sirc, G. (1989). Response in the electronic medium. In C. Anson (Ed.), *Writing and response: Theory, practice, and research* (pp. 187-205). Urbana, IL: National Council of Teachers of English.

Smart, G. (1999). Storytelling in a central bank: The role of narrative in the creation and use of specialized economic knowledge. *Journal of Business and Technical Communication, 13*(3), 249-273.

Smith, D. E. (1984). Textually mediated social organization. *International Social Science Journal, 34*, 59-75.

Spilka, R. (1990). Orality and literacy in the workplace: Process- and text-based strategies for multiple audience adaptation. *Journal of Business and Technical Communication, 4*(1), 44-67.

Spinuzzi, C. (2003). *Tracing genres through organizations: A sociocultural approach to information design*. Cambridge, MA: Massachusetts Institute of Technology Press.

Spinuzzi, C., and Zachary, M. (2000). Genre ecologies: An open-system approach to understanding and constructing documentation. *ACM Journal of Computer Documentation, 24*(3), 169-181.

Star, S. L., and Griesemer, J. R. (1989). Institutional ecology, 'translations' and boundary objects: Amateurs and professionals in Berkeley's Museum of Vertebrate Zoology, 1907-39. *Social Studies of Science, 19*, 387-420.

Suchman, L. A. (1987). *Plans and situated actions: The problem of human machine communication*. New York: Cambridge University Press.

Swales, J. M. (1990). *Genre analysis: English in academic and research settings*. New York: Cambridge University Press.

Swarts, H., Flower, L., and Hayes, J. R. (1984). Designing protocol studies of the writing process: An introduction. In R. Beach and L. Bidwell (Eds.), *New Directions in Composition Research* (pp. 53-71). New York: Guilford Press.

Swarts, J. (2002). *Textual replay mediation of writing reviews: Developing technology to afford enculturation.* Unpublished doctoral dissertation. Rensselaer Polytechnic Institute, Troy, NY.

Swarts, J. (2004a). Technological mediation of document review: The use of textual replay in two organizations. *Journal of Business and Technical Communication, 18*(3), 328-360.

Swarts, J. (2004b). Textual grounding: How people turn texts into tools. *Journal of Technical Writing and Communication, 34*(1), 67-89.

Taylor, F. W. (1911/1967). *The principles of scientific management.* New York: Norton Library.

van der Geest, T., and van Gemert, L. (1997). Review as a method for improving professional texts. *Journal of Business and Technical Communication, 11*(4), 433-450.

Vincent, D. (1993). *Literacy and popular culture: England 1750-1914.* New York: Cambridge University Press.

Vygotsky, L. S. (1978). *Mind in society: The development of higher psychological processes.* Cambridge, MA: Harvard University Press.

Whittaker, S. (1995). Rethinking video as a technology for interpersonal communications: Theory and design implications. *International Journal of Human-Computer Studies, 42,* 501-529.

Winsor, D. (1996). *Writing like an engineer.* Mahwah, NJ: Lawrence Erlbaum Associates.

Winsor, D. A. (2001). Learning to do knowledge work in systems of distributed cognition. *Journal of Business and Technical Communication, 15*(1), 5-28.

Wood, C. C. (1992a). *A cultural-cognitive approach to collaborative writing (CSRP 242).* Brighton, UK: University of Sussex.

Wood, C. C. (1992b). *A study of the graphical mediating representations used by collaborating authors (CSRP 230).* Brighton, UK: University of Sussex.

Yates, J. (1993). *Control through communications: The rise of system in American management.* Baltimore, MD: Johns Hopkins University Press.

Yates, J., and Orlikowski, W. (1994). Genre repertoire: The structuring of communicative practices in organizations. *Administrative Science Quarterly, 39*(4), 541-574.

Yates, J., and Orlikowski, W. (2002). Genre systems: Structuring interaction through communicative norms. *Journal of Business Communication, 39*(1), 13-35.

Young, R. (1978). Paradigms and problems: Needed research in rhetorical invention. In C. Cooper and L. Odell (Eds.), *Research in composing* (pp. 29-47). Urbana, IL: National Council of Teachers of English.

Index

For further ordering queries and information please contact our
Headquarters office: Taylor & Francis Group, an Informa business,
Verlag GmbH, Bottlingerstr. 66, 53173 Bonn, Germany.